Queering Wesley, Queering the Church

QUEERING WESLEY,
QUEERING THE CHURCH

Keegan Osinski

CASCADE *Books* • Eugene, Oregon

QUEERING WESLEY, QUEERING THE CHURCH

Cascade Books
An Imprint of Wipf and Stock Publishers
199 W. 8th Ave., Suite 3
Eugene, OR 97401

www.wipfandstock.com

PAPERBACK ISBN: 978-1-7252-5403-9
HARDCOVER ISBN: 978-1-7252-5404-6
EBOOK ISBN: 978-1-7252-5405-3

Cataloguing-in-Publication data:

Names: Osinski, Keegan, author.

Title: Queering Wesley, queering the church / Keegan Osinski.

Description: Eugene, OR : Cascade Books, 2021 | Includes bibliographical references.

Identifiers: ISBN x978-1-7252-5403-9 (paperback) | ISBN 978-1-7252-5404-6 (hardcover) | ISBN 978-1-7252-5405-3 (ebook)

Subjects: LCSH: Queer theology. | Wesley, John, 1703–1791. | Methodist Church—Doctrines. | Theology, Doctrinal.

Classification: BT83.65 .O85 2021 (paperback) | BT83.65 .O85 (ebook)

07/07/21

A version of the chapter "Circumcision of the Heart" originally appeared in *Methodist Revolutions: Evangelical Engagements of Church and World,* Joerg Rieger and Upolu Luma Vaai, general editors, GBHEM Publishing, 2021. Used with permission.

To the queer Nazarenes—past, present, and future.

CONTENTS

ACKNOWLEDGMENTS

It takes a village to make a book, and I am so grateful for the village of people who loved this one out of me.

To the Wesleyan Theological Society, for their willingness to hear early versions of some chapters and to discuss the need for this book in the world. Thank you.

To my pastors at Blakemore Church of the Nazarene: Dana Preusch, Ryan Hansen, and Christa Klosterman, for giving me a safe and welcoming place to worship and serve over the years. Thank you.

To the School of Theology and Christian Ministry and the Wesleyan Center at Point Loma Nazarene University, for their encouragement and support for this project and for my entire life. To Sam Powell and Michael Lodahl, who must take the credit and the blame for much of my work, because without them I very truly would not be here. The depth of my love and appreciation is endless. Particularly Dr. Powell, who, once upon receiving an email that said, "I remember you telling a story about Wesley and grapes???" replied with the primary source I needed within two minutes. To Mark Maddix and Ron Benefiel, for doing the hard things that I didn't even have to know about. To Rob Thompson, for care, space, and pretzels. Thank you.

To my Vanderbilt Divinity Library colleagues, for their patience and encouragement while I always had this book on my brain. Especially Bill Hook and Bobby Smiley, supervisors who trusted me and gave me space and time to do this work—part of being a scholar-librarian! Thank you.

To Ellen Armour, for reading the very first beginnings of this project, for shepherding the pieces that became my Master's thesis, for convincing me it was good, and for telling me I could do it without a PhD. Thank you.

To Joerg Rieger, for reminding me that there *are* progressive Wesleyans and for helping me find them. For reading drafts and pointing me in the right direction. For inviting me into this project that is bigger than any of us. Thank you.

To Tom Oord, for introducing me to my editor, Charlie, and for courageously paving the way for me and other progressive Nazarenes, for being a sounding board, discussion partner, and source of encouragement always, and for being a model of Wesleyan charity. Thank you.

To the Solises and the rest of my Tempo Nashville family, for keeping me caffeinated and full of breakfast tacos and love. Thank you.

To my weird and wonderful community on Twitter, for putting up with my agonizingly whiny writing progress and cheering for me the whole time. Thank you.

INTRODUCTION

In a moment where the influence, involvement, and even existence of LGBTQ+ Christians in the Wesleyan tradition are in question and in jeopardy, a reading of John Wesley that takes seriously his work and legacy as well as the concerns and experiences of queer people is sorely needed. It is imperative that Wesleyans acknowledge that the queer perspective has something important to offer the church, and that it is consistent with the broader thrust of Wesleyan theology and practice. Precious little work has been done to bring together queer theory and Wesleyan theology. Bringing such a perspective into the Wesleyan churches will richen the conversation, which is so often *about* LGBTQ+ Christians rather than explored *with* them or led *by* them. By demonstrating how John Wesley's sermons can lend themselves to a liberatory queer reading, I hope to show that the Wesleyan tradition can be a fertile and hospitable home for a queer theology that is consistent with a doctrine of holiness and other Wesleyan values.

This project begins with this introductory chapter that situates my argument in context, defines relevant terms and method, and lays out the reasoning and warrants for such a use of John Wesley and an understanding of queerness as a boon to holiness rather than an impediment. It is followed by queer readings of ten of John Wesley's sermons. These readings will explore the text of the sermons from a queer perspective, reading them with an eye toward questions of gender and sexuality that, while perhaps not explicit or intended in their original context, nevertheless have relevance and import to today's Wesleyan Christians.

First, some necessary definitions. In this book, I use "queer" as an adjective to signify that which is not normative, particularly as relating to sex, gender, and sexuality and the expressions thereof. That is, what is queer resists a biological essentialism of sex, the gender binary, and assumed or required heterosexuality. "Queer" is often used as a shorthand, catchall term for the LGBTQ+[1] community, that is, lesbian, gay, bisexual, and transgender people, as well as intersex, asexual, pansexual, and other non-heterosexual and non-gender-conforming identities. It also includes the disruption of political aspects of gender and sexuality norms, including marriage, monogamy, child rearing, and family building. The reclaiming of "queer" from those who would use it as a slur demonstrates exactly the queer refusal to be labeled, boxed in, and rendered inert.

Episcopal priest Elizabeth Edman uses "queer" to signify "something that has at its center an impulse to disrupt any and all efforts to reduce into simplistic dualisms our experience of life" and goes on to discuss queer theory and its "urgent need to rupture, or disrupt, binary thinking about gender and sexual identity."[2] The queer resists a static, monadic model of the world and human life, and insists on a more nuanced, complex, ecstatic vision, full of possibility and without limitation. The queer refuses to settle for a single possible narrative. Queerness chafes and bristles at the starched collars of compulsory structures, yearning to stretch and spin and bend and breathe. It shakes off synthetic shoulds in favor of searching for what is indelibly authentic and true.

It is worth noting, however, that not all LGBTQ+ individuals are comfortable with the word "queer" or choose to reclaim it for their own identification. It can still do harm, even when used with positive connotations and intentions. For this reason, using the term as a catchall for others or using the term as a cisgender heterosexual person can sometimes be offensive. As with any group of people, the LGBTQ+ community is not a monolith, and each person has their own opinions and expressions of their sexuality and identity and the language they prefer when defining it. In conversation and relationship, it is always better to ask than to assume and to use the words your friends prefer for themselves.

I use "queer" as a verb to mean engaging in the practice of problematizing normative narratives and assumptions—to fuck with those givens

---

1. There are many renderings of this acronym, the most common being LGBT, which serves to identify the community of Lesbian, Gay, Bisexual, and Transgender people. I choose to expand it with the addition of the letter Q, signifying Queer (often it also signifies Questioning for those exploring their sexuality or gender), which may have numerous additional significations, for gender and sexuality, biology and politics. I also choose to include the "+" to signify the panoply of other discrete identities, such as Intersex, Asexual, and others, which deserve recognition, but which would be impossible to list upon each mention.

2. Edman, *Queer Virtue*, 3–4.

that perpetuate the power structures that baptize and uphold some norms while damning and marginalizing alternative ways of being. It is the active pursuit of the disruption of the *status quo* and normative ways of being. It takes what is given and questions its validity, its application, its implications. It injects the wisdom and experience of queer life into whatever subject is at hand. It asks, "Why?" and also, "Why not?" To queer the church is to inject it with the vibrant sexual and gender diversity that reflects the variant multiplicity of the God who created and sustains in love all of God's diverse creation.

I define a "queer reading" as an attempt to queer—that is, disrupt and interrogate the sex, gender, and sexuality norms of—a given text. To read queerly is to look at a text from different angles and through different eyes, to see what's missing or what takes up too much space, to explore all the possibilities of what the text could be saying, and to tease out what might be hiding closeted within the text. Queer reading has been a tool in the belt of literary theory since it collided with the ascent of queer theory in the 1970s. Queer literary theory expands the possible readings and ways to understand a text in terms of the assumptions of gender and sexuality inherent in the text either explicitly or under the surface.[3] Even in texts that do not explicitly deal with sexuality or gender, we find sexual undercurrents always at play, for all of life is shot through with *eros*, and nothing we do is left untouched by the materiality of our gendered socialization.

The history of language regarding LGBTQ+ roles, identities, activities, and subcultures is rich and extensive. For more information on the term "queer" and its use in the social construction of homosexuality and LGBTQ+ culture, see Rictor Norton's *Myth of the Modern Homosexual* as well as George Chauncey's *Gay New York*.

Very little work has been done at the intersection of Wesleyan studies and queer theory. There are several reasons for this major gap. One is the historical lack of support and affirmation for LGBTQ+ persons in the Wesleyan tradition. As of this writing, no Wesleyan denomination is unequivocally open and affirming in its polity. The closest thing to an affirming Wesleyan organization is the United Methodist Church's Reconciling

---

3. Berthold Schoene credits especially Michel Foucault's *History of Sexuality* as foundational in establishing queerness as an identity and methodology that "designates at once an indeterminate and open signifier, which is both singular and infinitely plural, and a quite definitive political stance, which is grassroots-political and pragmatic as well as utopia-bound." See Schoene, "Queer Politics, Queer Theory, and the Future of 'Identity.'"

Ministries Network, an organization not officially affiliated with the UMC that educates and equips churches and individuals in creating affirming church spaces with concern for various intersections of oppression, including gender and sexuality, in ways that are specifically and self-consciously faithful to a Wesleyan theology and ethic. The RMN links individual congregations that "have approved a statement that specifically names a welcome of people of all sexual orientations and gender identities." This kind of statement from individual churches is necessary, the RMN website says, "because our United Methodist Church holds official policies that exclude LGBTQ people from the life of the Church."[4] There are hundreds of congregations associated with the RMN, but the United Methodist Church itself is split on whether the denomination as a whole should become affirming.[5] This split opinion may indeed result eventually in a formal split of the UMC. So while there are LGBTQ+ Wesleyans and allies—laity, clergy, and scholars—who are working hard for the inclusion of queer people in the Wesleyan churches, in most contexts they speak out usually only at great risk to their reputations, communities, livelihoods, or even lives. More likely, they don't speak out at all, especially in more conservative denominations or geographical areas. Therefore, little formal or scholarly work has been done to construct a queer Wesleyan theology.

Pamela Lightsey's *Our Lives Matter* is the first major published work integrating Wesleyan theology with a constructive theology specifically concerned about the intersectional issues of race, class, gender, and sexuality. Lightsey was the first out black female clergy in the United Methodist Church, and her book presents a queer womanist theology framed by the 2014 riots in Ferguson, Missouri, that is thoroughly Wesleyan. She explains that "queering, as a theological methodology, is a deconstruction and re-evaluation of gender perspectives that uses as its framework queer theory

4. See the RMN website: RMNetwork.org.

5. The weekend I completed writing this chapter, delegates of the UMC met at a special session of General Conference to vote on the church's policies on LGBTQ+ inclusion. Several "plans" were proposed, including the One Church Plan, in which the policy remained ambiguous and individual congregations could decide for themselves whether they would be affirming or not; and the Traditional Plan, in which the policy was made more clearly unaffirming. The delegation voted to pass the Traditional Plan. The official statement released by the UMC says that "the changes proposed by the Traditional Plan are mostly about ordination of LGBTQ clergy and how to resolve issues when a clergy violates our human sexuality stances by, for example, performing a same-sex marriage." See Iovino, "What Happened and What Didn't at General Conference 2019."

and as its resources scripture, reason, tradition, and experience."[6] She evokes a queered version of the so-called Wesleyan Quadrilateral—the well-loved and oft-cited framework for evaluating authority within Wesleyan traditions, which I will discuss further below—that centers the queer reading of Scripture, and the reason, tradition, and experience of queer people.

The UMC's first openly lesbian bishop, Karen Oliveto, has also done some apologetic work to shed light on the experiences of queer people in the church. Her book *Together at the Table*[7] shares her personal story and uses it as a springboard to discuss the existence of sexual diversity and inclusion in the church and the need for the church to recognize and celebrate it. In *Our Strangely Warmed Hearts*, Bishop Oliveto continues to use personal narratives to bolster the same argument. She also traces LGBTQ+ history more broadly in order to situate the UMC within it and interrogate the way the UMC has responded to the LGBTQ+ people in its own flock. She stresses the need for the cis-hetero-dominant UMC to dialog with and defer to its LGBTQ+ members and clergy, to engage them as a valid and vital part of the denomination that should be leading the denomination's policy and work regarding LGBTQ+ issues, for they are the ones whose careers, faith, and indeed lives are at stake.

Where the Wesleyan tradition unfortunately lacks any robust queer interpretation, queer theory as a discipline, rooted in the literary theory and specifically deconstruction of the late-twentieth century, provides abundant tools for application across fields. Judith Butler and her historical work *Gender Trouble* did eminently important work in laying the foundation for thinking of gender along Foucaultian lines as performative rather than essential or biologically based. Religious studies has taken up queer theory not only as a method of reading texts, but also as a method of doing de/constructive theology. Mark Jordan's 2001 *The Ethics of Sex* employs queer theory and historical studies to understand the state of Christian sexual ethics and make a case for a broader inclusion of queer experience as Christian experience. Marcella Althaus-Reid's work queers liberation theology, pushing provocatively for an "indecenting" of theology that exposes and opens up Christian thought to the real lives of poor, queer women, who she argues have much to offer to the work of theology. In the realm of practical

6. Lightsey, *Our Lives Matter*, 27.

7. It is perhaps interesting to note that, while *Our Strangely Warmed Hearts* was published by Abingdon, which is a UMC publishing house, *Together at the Table* was published by Westminster John Knox Press, which is owned by the Presbyterian Publishing Corporation.

theology, an increasing number of ministers and lay-theologians alike have done work towards normalizing, celebrating, and taking seriously queer experience as source material for doing theology and making the church, broadly considered and across denominational lines, a more welcoming place for all kinds of people. Books such as Patrick Cheng's *From Sin to Amazing Grace* and *Radical Love* are clear and accessible volumes that (re) frame theology through a queer lens but nonetheless remain faithful to the traditional doctrine and ethics of the church. Elizabeth Edman's *Queer Virtue* shows how queer life is not only compatible with Christian life, but that the church can indeed be enlivened and revitalized by considering as instructive the practice and ethics of LGBTQ+ people.

While much scholarly and practical work is being done in the area of queer theology, very little of it is coming out of or speaking directly to the Wesleyan tradition. Not only is this unfortunate for the Wesleyan denominations, but it is also puzzling, given what I find to be ample resonance between John Wesley's *ethos*, the work and witness of Wesleyan churches, and the doctrines, traditions, and practices we hold dear, and the possibilities revealed to us by queer experience and thought. Therefore, I hope to offer my voice as a queer member of the Church of the Nazarene to connect these dots and provide this creative connection that is sorely needed.

The Wesleyan tradition uses its founder as a resource for constructive theology in a variety of ways and for a variety of issues. Because of the general openness and generosity inherent in Wesley's thought as a whole, Wesleyan theologians have appealed to him as a source as they argue for a properly Christian response to the poor, labor, the body, and women, to give a few examples.[8] In all of these cases, contemporary thinkers use an eighteenth-century Wesley to address current needs of the church and society, even though this is not without its challenges and pitfalls. Many of these same challenges and pitfalls crop up when using the ancient documents of the Bible to address current needs as well. Feminist Wesleyan theologians, for example, emphasize Wesley's encouragement of women in ministry and paint him as a kind of proto-feminist egalitarian,[9] though of course he was a man of his time. Nevertheless, the spirit of Wesley's work does lend itself

---

8. Manfred Marquardt's *John Wesley's Social Ethics* covers such areas of Wesley's own specific social praxis as poverty, education, slavery, and prisons, in order to argue that Wesley and Methodism's influence was beyond the spiritual and religious but also importantly geared toward social ethics. Wesleyans have naturally taken this social consciousness and expanded it to apply to other contemporary issues.

9. See, for example, Leclerc, *Singleness of Heart*.

to a feminist reading, such that a feminist Wesleyan position is not only possible and tenable, but indeed robust and faithful, as well as increasingly popular. I contend that the same can be said for a queer reading of Wesley. I am under no illusions that John Wesley himself had any liberatory sense of sexuality or premonitions of gender-bent holiness, but as an heir to his legacy, a fish in the stream of his tradition, I have the privilege of using what I have been given in his words to think with the current and in tandem with all the resources that have come after him to address the present in an adequate and relevant manner.

One such legacy resource of the Wesleyan tradition is the so-called Wesleyan Quadrilateral. This conceptual tool asserts that there are four essential resources available for thinking through matters of faith: Scripture, Reason, Experience, and Tradition. Further, each of these resources is on more or less equal footing with the others. Wesleyans do not hold the *sola scriptura* of other traditions, but assert that Scripture has as much purchase in the church and the individual's understanding of God and the Christian life as one's own experience. In fact, researcher of religion Dawne Moon, in her work studying Methodist congregations, found that experience plays a hugely influential role in the way people understand Scripture. Their everyday theologies affected what they took Scripture to say. "Although members also saw their beliefs about homosexuality as following from their theologies," Moon says, "in fact beliefs about and experiences with homosexuality, lesbians and gay men, often shaped people's understandings about who God is and what God intends for people. These beliefs and experiences could even shape how members understood Scripture."[10] Reason, that is, a philosophical logic or a new scientific explanation, holds just as much weight as the traditional way things have "always" been done. Again, Moon finds that a presentation of theology and Scripture must mesh with one's experience and understanding of reality in order for it to take. She explains that "it was impossible for [people] to believe things about Scripture that went against what they already knew about God and life—interpretations of Scripture had to *make sense*."[11] The framework of the Quadrilateral, so prized and oft touted in the Wesleyan tradition, gives ample space for the creative use of queer thinking to inform our faith and practice. Giving power and authority to queer experience is one of the most important things

10. Moon, *God, Sex, and Politics*, 57.

11. Moon, *God, Sex, and Politics*, 63.

we can do at this juncture to move our understanding of faith forward into new and vital possibilities for the future of the church.

Perhaps the most important and unique identifying characteristic of Wesleyan theology is the primacy of *holiness*. In his compendium of Wesleyan theology, J. Kenneth Grider relays how "Wesleyans for well over 100 years have been known as the Holiness people. The Wesleyan denominations have been known as Holiness churches, their preachers as Holiness clergy. The ongoing life and work of these churches has been known as the Holiness Movement."[12] Holiness is truly the key to Wesley's thought and the life of the Wesleyan churches. Therefore, queering Wesley will require a serious consideration of holiness: How is holiness compatible with queerness? What does queerness contribute to holiness? What is holy about being queer? What is queer about being holy?

The historical development of the doctrine of Wesleyan holiness is a good place to start, and it leaves us both a solid foundation on which we can build and an expansive openness into which we can grow. For the tradition of holiness is not only one thing, but has been stretched and molded over time by a variety of voices, each with their own unique contributions, and it leans into the future, inviting us to consider it anew.

Beginning with Paul Culbertson's psychologically based reading of holiness in the 1960s, Nazarene theologians, and other Wesleyans as well, began exploring what Samuel Powell calls "the possibility of alternative interpretations of holiness."[13] Previous to this period, the Wesleyan tradition generally had been content to more or less agree on a single, traditional understanding of holiness that was considered standard. However, through the broader cultural tumult of the 1970s and 1980s, Nazarenes Mildred Bangs Wynkoop and Rob Staples, as well as others, reimagined the consensus on holiness. Whereas previously it was understood as a single moment of the eradication of sin, the baptism with the Holy Spirit, and entire sanctification, the new interpretations focused primarily on love and relationality with God and neighbor as the core of holiness. These burgeoning ways of thinking about holiness were not without their challengers. Traditionalists insisted that to change the terminology or interpretation of holiness would result in a complete crumbling of the doctrine that elevated human work and will and rendered God only marginally engaged in sanctification. The rise of these new readings of holiness and the challenges to them put

12. Grider, *Wesleyan-Holiness Theology*, 371.

13. Powell, *Holiness in the 21st Century*, 9.

on display the fact that, while there had been something of an agreement on the doctrine of holiness, in truth there had always been a diversity of understandings at play in the tradition. Powell explains that this diversity "lent credence to the endeavors of Wynkoop, Staples and others. If there was already a range of views in the tradition from its beginning, then there could be no principled objection to Wynkoop's adding to the mixture."[14] The preexisting variety of Wesleyan conceptions of holiness was an invitation to additional creativity in reading the doctrine in light of tradition, culture, and the works of John Wesley himself.

The Wesleyan tradition is at a place now where it is again time for more new interpretations of holiness. While there are still traditionalists who worry about what a new reading will mean or do within the church, we have seen that faithful interpretation is not only one thing. There is room for new readings, ones that open up the possibilities of the wonder and diversity of God and God's multitudes, which manifest in the lives and faces of humanity. To read holiness anew is not to abolish the wisdom of the doctrine so dear to us Wesleyans, but rather to breathe new life into it so that it might be enjoyed and lauded for another generation and understood in a way that is fresh and relevant to our world today. Wynkoop insists that if Wesley "is to speak to us in our day, some method of interpretation will be needed to bridge over the historical changes that separate us."[15] This was the case for her in 1972, and it is the case for us today. New interpretations are needed to bridge even the changes since Wynkoop's writing. And yet such an interpretation will not be "a setter forth of new doctrines," as Wesley said Christian essentials are sometimes received, but will preach only "Jesus and the resurrection."[16] New readings can pick up where old ones left off, without leaving the tradition and legacy behind completely. In fact, that tradition and legacy is what makes the new readings possible at all.

The new reading of holiness presented in this book is one that includes queerness. Indeed, it puts queerness to work, building out Wesleyan holiness with factors that exist within the queer experience and lend themselves to thinking about holiness in a more expansive way than it can be when limited to a binary, heteronormative framework. The LGBTQ+ community has its own set of values and motivations that can help us envision holiness more richly. Elizabeth Edman says that "Queer ethical demands

14. Powell, *Holiness in the 21st Century*, 11.

15. Wynkoop, *Theology of Love*, 77.

16. Wesley, *Works* 1:401.

clearly and often exquisitely manifest widely recognized Christian virtues: spiritual discernment, rigorous self-assessment, honesty, courage, material risk, dedication to community life, and care for the marginalized and oppressed."[17] Applying these virtues to think about holiness specifically will broaden the conversation in a way that enriches the life of the church and the lives of individual Christians, both cisgender[18] heterosexual and not.

The potential problems that worry some traditionalists about the inclusion of LGBTQ+ people in church and in theology are far outweighed by the potential benefits, and indeed in many cases such problems are not truly problems at all. I am not interested here in arguing whether queer identity or sex or "lifestyle" are sinful, or whether a "self-avowed practicing homosexual" can be a Christian. I am not interested in discussing the biblical text and whether it supports or condemns homosexuality or the gender binary. Others have done this work with varying success in terms of analysis and persuasion.[19] Instead, I am working under some given assumptions, which here will not be up for debate: LGBTQ+ Christians are Christians. Queerness does not preclude one from being a Christian. Attraction to or sex with one's own gender is not, in itself, sin. As Christians, LGBTQ+ people experience God and God's revelation in unique ways, and have their own gifts to offer the church if the church would only receive them.

Wynkoop says that "the summarizing word—Wesley's ultimate hermeneutic—is *love*. Every strand of his thought, the warm heart of every doctrine, the passion of every sermon, the test of every claim to Christian grace, was love," and that "so central is love that to be 'Wesleyan' is to be committed to a theology of love."[20] It is time for the Wesleyan churches to recognize that love takes all kinds of shapes, exists in all sizes, in all colors and places and permutations. To limit our understanding of love to the heterosexual, or worse, to the disembodied unsexed spiritual milquetoast of sentimentality, is to limit the God who is love to the same. The queer love of gay men and lesbians, of bi- and pansexuals, of transgender, intersex, and asexual folks displays the vibrant diversity of love that reveals who God

---

17. Edman, *Queer Virtue*, 3.

18. To be "cisgender" is to identify as the same gender one was assigned at birth. "Cis" is a Latin prefix meaning "same."

19. See, for example, Wink, "Biblical Perspectives on Homosexuality," and Jordan, *Invention of Sodomy in Christian Theology*, both of which will be discussed in later chapters.

20. Wynkoop, *Theology of Love*, 101.

is, that manifests God in the flesh and blood and sweat and tears of every human being made in God's image.

The heart of Wesleyan holiness is perfect love of God and neighbor. There is nothing inherent in LGBTQ+ life that precludes either of these things, and in fact there are ways that queer experience provides unique insight and guidance toward these goals. There is an intrinsic identification of queer people with Jesus—the singular human embodiment of God on earth was disregarded, disrespected, and discredited in much the same ways queer people are marginalized, and yet his non-normative life and love is the example *par excellence* of holiness and Christian perfection. Patrick Cheng draws this connection in his work, *From Sin to Amazing Grace*, when he outlines different aspects of Christ as models for understanding the holiness of queer Christian experience. For example, beginning with Jesus' statement that "whoever does the will of my Father in heaven is my brother and sister and mother" (Matt 12:50), Christians have formed creative family units, refusing to be bound by biology or caste in a way that is mirrored by the queer construction of "chosen families" that engender profound care and support where there otherwise is none. The process of coming out, of confronting the truth of who one is and how one must move through the world so as to exist honestly, finds resonance in the Christian practices of self-reflection, confrontation of sin, repentance, and recognition of the *imago dei* in humanity.

These themes, and others, reveal themselves in Wesley's sermons, and reading these sermons with a queer eye from a queer experience will draw out the connections that show queerness to be not only compatible with holiness freshly understood, but also a truly fruitful and beneficial piece of a broader picture of what holiness is and can be. John Wesley is still an important and valuable resource for churches in the Wesleyan tradition, and Wesleyan theology can use his work to push forward toward a future in which the church is a site of wholeness, love, and liberation for queer people who seek to embody his vision of holiness. A queer reading of John Wesley's sermons is just the beginning of the generative possibilities of queering Wesley, queering the church.

NOTE ON SELECTION

Attraction can be surprising. Particularly when it's queer, when it's out of order, when it's *forbidden*. That jolt in the stomach, that tingle at the back of the neck that finds its way to the jaw and the tongue that wonders what theirs might taste like. That glance that is caught and eyes that lock across a room where no one else notices. In a world of compulsory heterosexuality, that queer spark of attraction can be an unexpected thrill. To welcome it with joy and curiosity and compassion is to practice hospitality toward self and others. To repress and shame and excise it is to sin.

Perhaps queer love is like treasure hidden in a field, which a man found and hid; and for joy over it he goes and sells all that he has and buys that field. When you encounter the surprise of queer love, consider it a treasure and invest in it. See what it might yield.

This unexpected mystery of queer attraction has been my guiding principle in selecting the ten sermons in this book. As I read the words of John Wesley, sifting through them, turning them over with my mind and my fingers, occasionally I would discover a sparkle of treasure, a jolt of attraction, and I'd run with it. I found that some sermons just *felt* queer— they gave me that knowing nod, that just-long-enough eye contact that signals—what exactly? A potentiality. A curiosity. A *desire*. Many colleagues and friends posed the question to me: Why *these* sermons? How did you choose them? I had hoped to have some sort of structured methodology with which to select the sermons to explore, or at least some process I could explain or report. But as is often the case when dealing with the vagaries of queerness, no such organized procedure has been followed. As Lea Brown says in her essay on kinky domination and submission play, "Sexual desire is irrational and unpredictable. We do not know what creates and stimulates desire within an individual."[21] Such was my experience being enticed by these sermons.

To find what's queer in John Wesley's self-consciously chaste and decidedly unsexual sermons from a time and place so far from our current understandings of gender and sexuality was quite the adventure. But as a queer person living in a straight society, it's not one I'm unfamiliar with. Finding resonances in a world and a church that was not made for you is the daily work of LGBTQ+ people. The good news is "Seek, and ye shall find." I was not disappointed in my reading of Wesley, and to find these queer resonances in his work is to open up Wesleyan theology to a new time and culture, a new church of queer Christians who are seeking the holiness he so unfailingly preached about. The fruit is there if we seek it. If we pay attention to the subtle touch, the wink of queerness latent in the

---

21. Brown, "Dancing in the Eros of Domination and Submission," 149.

Wesleyan tradition and in the world itself, we might catch that surprising attraction of the queer spark.

A NOTE ON READING

It was not practical or even feasible to include the entirety of the sermon texts in this volume. I do quote them extensively from Albert Outler's volumes of the Abingdon edition of Wesley's Works (from which I also take the sermon dates), however it will most likely be helpful to have copies of the sermons to read side-by-side with these chapters to provide greater context and to allow you to perhaps exercise your own creative readings of the primary sources. Online versions are available on the Northwest Nazarene University Wesley Center website (wesley.nnu.edu) as well as the Wesleyan Holiness Digital Library (whdl.org).

Unless otherwise noted, all of Wesley's works are quoted from the Abingdon Bicentennial Edition of *The Works of John Wesley*, edited by Richard Heitzenrater, Randy Maddox, and Frank Baker, which I have abbreviated in citations as *Works*.

THE NEW BIRTH

In his sermon, "The New Birth," John Wesley uses the text from John 3, the story of Nicodemus seeking out Jesus at night, to give what he believes to be a "full and clear account" of people's need to be "born again," and what that looks like in the Christian life. Jesus tells Nicodemus that one must be born again in order to see the Kingdom of God, and Nicodemus asks earnestly, "How can someone be born when they are old?" (John 3:3–4). The why and how of this strange but necessary New Birth is the subject of this sermon.

Wesley's sermon asks and answers three questions:

1. Why must we be born again? Or: What's wrong with how things are?

2. How must we be born again? Or: What does being born again look like?

3. To what end must we be born again? Or: What's the outcome of being born again?

I will consider each portion of the sermon, reading this sermon with a queer framework that reads "New Birth" as a kind of "coming out": A movement from a life of wrong-headed wrongdoing into the fullness of life promised and gifted by God.

Along with the doctrine of justification, Wesley says that the New Birth is one of two doctrines that "within the whole compass of Christianity may be properly termed fundamental."[1] Being born again, emerging into a new kind of life that reflects more truly the complete and restored image of God, is the most bedrock, foundational aspect of Wesley's holiness and Christianity as a whole. Everything else—works of piety, works of mercy, sanctification—is all secondary and dependent upon the New Birth.

1. Wesley, *Works* 2:187.

The New Birth marks the beginning, the fresh opening of opportunity and possibility that would otherwise be out of reach. In the moment of New Birth, God's Spirit "works in our hearts" and "renews our fallen nature."[2] The Holy Spirit works in us to birth a new self, free from our old, harmful, unhealthy ways of being that reveal the worst inclinations of humanity.

For queer folks, coming out can be exactly this kind of renewal of a life formerly marked by a "fallen nature"—the inability to see and love oneself for who one is, usually caused or at least influenced by negative talk and ideology from family or other communities; repression of desires rather than addressing or otherwise processing them, which can lead to dysfunction and harmful acting out; lying about some of the most important, essential aspects of one's being. By claiming one's identity and desires in an act of coming out—to oneself or others—a person can experience a release from all of these sins and begin a new kind of life marked by wholeness and holiness rather than secrecy and shame.

A coming out event can take many forms. It can be deeply personal and private, an internal reflection or realization within oneself, where one can honestly interrogate oneself, asking and answering questions that may be hard to ask, that may be forbidden or squashed, denied or hidden away. It can be a public occasion, sharing with parents, siblings, or other family members, with close friends, or with larger communities. It can be a pleasant, supportive, and empowering experience. But it can also be deeply painful, even scarring. Ultimately, though, whatever form a coming out may take, it signals the birth of a new life. Life changes, indelibly. The old passes away, and the new begins to emerge, an open slate, a possibility for freedom.

In *From Sin to Amazing Grace*, one of the models Patrick Cheng provides for the movement from sin to grace is that of the "Out Christ," wherein the sin is portrayed as the "closet" and the grace as coming out. He talks about the toxicity of being in the closet, how it "prevents a person from truly connecting with others" and how that "has a corrosive effect on the self-esteem and well-being" of people.[3] Sin is often described as "wrong relationship" with God or with others, and being in the closet is a fitting example of that. To choose, or be forced, to lie about who you are and who you love is a poor foundation for a healthy relationship with others and proves to have disastrous ramifications for one's own health and relationship

2. Wesley, *Works* 2:187.

3. Cheng, *From Sin to Amazing Grace*, 84.

with oneself as well. Cheng also describes the "sin of the closet" in terms of repression and the devastating results that repression can have when it bubbles up and lashes out in unforeseen and harmful ways.[4] The harm, dysfunction, and unhealth that are consequences of the sins of secrecy, shame, lying, and denial can only be counteracted by the grace of openness, honesty, and acceptance that result from coming out—from being born again. The "Out Christ" is the model for entering into this grace: it "reflects the very nature of a God who is also constantly coming out and revealing Godself to us."[5] Queer people also, in their coming out, can reclaim their own image of God, which Wesley says is lost in the fall of sin. By laying claim to the grace offered to them in coming out, LGBTQ+ persons can share and proclaim the image of God made fresh within them and share that holy, made-whole image with others. The grace or New Birth of coming out is, Cheng says, a gift from God, not only for the queer person, but also to those around them who are freed from the sins of the closet that affect them too. Coming out is a birth into a new life of grace in which the sins of the closet are healed and redeemed.

Wesley's short answer to the question "Why must we be born again?" is original sin. Because of Adam, Wesley says, "every man born into the world now bears the image of the devil in pride and self-will; the image of the beast, in sensual appetites and desires."[6] And because every person is born in sin, they must be born again in God, in Spirit, in righteousness.

Wesley's hamartiology is based on his understanding of the image of God in humanity and its subsequent loss as a result of the first humans' sin. The image of God is revealed in three categories: natural image, political image, and moral image. The natural image is humanity's spiritual nature, resultant from God's nature as spirit. The political image is humanity's ability and desire for organization and dominion. And the moral image—the one most integral in understanding morality and sin—is humanity's capacity for righteousness and holiness, that is, in Wesley's estimation, love.[7] Wesley says that "man at his creation was full of love; which was the sole principle of all his tempers, thoughts, words, and actions. God is full of justice, mercy, and truth; so was man as he came from the hands of his

---

4. Cheng, *From Sin to Amazing Grace*, 85.

5. Cheng, *From Sin to Amazing Grace*, 87.

6. Wesley, *Works* 2:190.

7. Wesley, *Works* 2:188.

Creator."[8] God's image as perfect love, which exists in and enlivens the first humans, is what is lost in sin.

J. Kenneth Grider addresses specifically Wesley's teaching on original sin. He asserts that we identify sin as sinful because it stands in contrast to God and God's holiness.[9] He says that for Wesley, "original sin is a state or condition that is, of course, relational—and that inclines us to acts of sin."[10] The inclination or tendency to act in unloving ways in our relationships, narrativized as a result of the rebellion of the first humans, is what is meant by original sin. It is a state of being rather than an act for which we are guilty. In fact, Wesley, along with Arminians generally, asserts that no one is culpable for the fact of their original sin, given the sacrifice of Christ's passion. Further, not only are we not culpable for our original sin, it is this state of being that Wesley believes we may be freed from by entire sanctification. Because of this distinction between state and act, Grider and others often prefer to talk about original sin in terms of "Adamic depravity" rather than "sin," for sin has come to signify a willful act of transgression rather than the inherent inclination toward unlove.

Therefore, the first human, as well as all of his offspring, were "now under the power of servile fear" rather than love.[11] It is this fear that drives us to the unlove of sin, of unloving and wrongheaded thinking of ourselves and others that forces us into ways of being that do not bring life but rather death. Because we have all been born into this sin, Wesley says, we must be born again.

Humanity, at its creation, was full of love, Wesley says. Having been made in the image[12] of God, love was "the sole principle of all [humanity's] tempers, thoughts, words, and actions."[13] To think of an ideal humanity, before the taint of sin, is to think a humanity whose primary mode of being, every thought, word, and deed, is love. Among other things, love must mean a holistic care and respect for persons. It also implies a simultaneous

8. Wesley, *Works* 9:47–48.

9. "Sin is sinful because God is holy," he says. Grider, *Wesleyan-Holiness Theology*, 257.

10. Grider, *Wesleyan-Holiness Theology*, 276.

11. Wesley, *Works* 2:189.

12. Here Wesley distinguishes between the natural, political, and moral images of God. The natural image is God's and humanity's spiritual being with feeling and will; the political image is God's and humanity's ability to rule and have dominion; and the moral image is God's and humanity's righteousness and holiness. It is the moral image which is *chief* in the conceptualization of the image of God according to Wesley.

13. Wesley, *Works* 2:188.

freedom to love without limit or condition. If love is the ultimate impetus and *telos* of every inter/action, who can say how that perfect love might be manifested? Certainly the perfect love of sinless humanity would be broader and deeper and bigger and *more* than the love we give or receive while limited by sin. To be free from the hurt and harm and shame of sin would surely result in a less restrictive love than we know today. Surely a perfect and limitless love would not be restricted exclusively to a vision of the heterosexual nuclear family. Surely the love envisioned in sinless perfection could be embodied in the lives of queer folks as well. To have love as the "sole principle" of all one's actions should be possible with any permutation of genitals and attractions.

In addition to thinking of the sin of the closet as dishonesty or wrong thinking of oneself, we might think of the sin of the closet as heteronormativity. To be "born into sin" is to be born into a heteronormative world, where queer people inherit a wrong view of ourselves as lesser, where we must sinfully will-to-power ourselves into straightness or gender conformity or limited views of what "love" looks like. This is, of course, not to say that being heterosexual is somehow more inherently sinful than being homo-, bi-, or a-sexual, but that the idea and enforced systems of compulsory heterosexuality—that heterosexuality is the default or should be normative or required or preferable—is. It is a force that distorts the image of God in others and results in oppression of those others and their consignment to suffering. In heteronormativity, we see the exercise of the "sensual appetites and desires" in the exertion of control and dominance over difference.

Being born anew by the Spirit of God into queer holiness/holy queerness would mean growing into our fullest selves, who God created us to be, properly reflecting the image of God in us, that is, perfect love. Coming out is a denunciation of domination, the refusal to be defined by the "image of the devil" that the original sin of heteronormativity and heterosexism has imposed on the queer person. It is a reclaiming of the pride that is closer to what Wesley calls humility—a right understanding of oneself.[14]

Next Wesley asks, how must we be born again? How, indeed? Wesley illustrates the function of being born again with the story of Jesus' encounter with Nicodemus in the Gospel of John.

---

14. I have a more extensive discussion of pride and humility in the chapter on Wesley's sermon, "Circumcision of the Heart."

This encounter in and of itself is quite queer. Nicodemus sneaks around at night hoping for a clandestine rendezvous with Jesus the rowdy rabble-rouser, the rebel challenging the social codes that give Nicodemus his social standing. The text sets up this dichotomy between Jesus and Nicodemus. Nicodemus, an established teacher in the community, seeks out Jesus to hear *his* teaching. We might read Nicodemus as engaging in the gay ritual of "cruising," visiting locations frequented by gay men in order to find sexual partners. It's almost too on-the-nose. How many times have we heard of the straight-laced anti-gay pastor, the family man with a secret Grindr account? Nicodemus knows that Jesus has that *something* that resonates with him, that he needs and is drawn to, but cannot quite pin down, and certainly not in broad daylight. Well-respected, well-to-do Nicodemus should have nothing to do with a Jesus-type besides utter rejection. His interest in Jesus is written in such a way that we can see a curiosity bubbling up from some repressed depths. Despite his resistance, his attraction to Jesus gets the better of him. And Nicodemus takes his first brave steps toward a New Birth by courageously following the lead of his desire.

"No one can see the kingdom of God," Jesus tells him, "unless they are born again" (John 3:3). Nicodemus is perplexed. Wesley asserts that the language of being "born again" would actually have been familiar to Nicodemus, as it was the custom of the Jews to baptize new believers—even adults—before circumcision, and that "when he was baptized, he was said to be born again; by which they meant, that he who was before a child of the devil was now adopted into the family of God."[15] But Nicodemus must have sensed that Jesus meant something else than this meaning to which he was accustomed. He must have *felt* it, known it deep within himself, the way he knew his desire to meet Jesus. He must have known it was something having to do with the groaning, painful, messy reality of literal birth, entangled with fluids and bellies and genitals. "*Surely* they cannot enter a second time into their mother's womb to be born!" Nicodemus scoffs, and you can almost hear a trailing hopeful incredulity: ". . . can they?" (John 3:4).

A further queerness apparent in this Nicodemus story is that we are to consider the imagery of birth, with its reliance on body parts typically assigned female, when no women are present in the story. The apparent necessity for these men to be subject to such "female" parts for salvation or fullness of life is reminiscent of the strange transgender promise of Jesus from the Gospel of Thomas that "every woman who has become male will

---

15. Wesley, *Works* 2:191.

enter the kingdom of heaven."[16] The gender requirements and consider-
ations of salvation seem muddled, fluid, confusing—very queer indeed. A
person is to be born again, born from above, born from the birth canal of
God, whom Jesus calls "Father." The functional details of this procedure are
anything but straightforward.

But the true answer to the "how" of the New Birth, according to Jesus,
is in the wind. The wind blows, and we can feel it, and we can hear it, but
we "cannot tell where it comes from or where it is going." It is a bit like por-
nography, in the sense that, like Supreme Court Justice Potter Stewart said,
it defies outright definition, but we know it when we see it. We can identify
the New Birth even if we are not sure whence it came.

In many formulations of salvation, the first step a person takes toward New Birth is repentance. Wesley says that to repent is to "know
yourselves."[17] Wesley means by this to know yourselves as sinners, specifically, but the more general point of squaring with who you truly are, what
you have done in the past, and what you hope and plan to do in the future is
well taken, with broader implications for being born again. Honest assessment of oneself is necessary for transformation.

Wesley uses the birth analogy to point out the difference between a
fetus and a child—the unborn human has eyes and ears, for example, but
cannot properly see or hear. The child who is born is able to make full
use of these capacities and truly live. In fact, Wesley says, "it is then only
when a [person] is born that we say, [they begin] to live."[18] The New Birth
of coming out can certainly feel like truly living for the first time. It can
be just as disorienting and traumatic as a true birth as well. But on the
other side is a life where all one's gifts and abilities can be exercised freely
and completely, without the dark, cramped quarters of a womb or a closet,
without the shame of dishonesty keeping vision obscured, without the sin
of heteronormativity denying the space to flourish.

The life of the New Birth is marked by a conspiring with—literally,
breathing with—God. Wesley says that in the new life born of the Spirit,

16. Gospel of Thomas Saying 114. In a strictly historical read, this demand is certainly
grounded in misogyny rather than any earnest embrace of gender bending, and perhaps
also contradicts the call for a person to truly know themselves as a prerequisite for New
Birth, but nonetheless any such implication and encouragement of gender fluidity in the
writings of the early church, even attributed to Christ himself, is worth interrogation
and play.

17. Wynkoop, *Theology of Love*, 153.

18. Wesley, *Works* 2:192.

"God is continually breathing, as it were, upon his soul, and his soul is breathing unto God."[19] The newly born, out person finds themselves face to face, mouth to mouth, with God, breathing in what God breathes out, and breathing out what God breathes back in. In the wake of the New Birth of coming out, we get to work with God from the liberated core of our truest selves to create a holy life we can be proud of. With God's help, we can breathe in the grace and hope and truth that is denied to us in the closet and breathe out love rather than sin.

Wesley says that the chief end of the New Birth is holiness, that is, "the image of God stamped upon the heart; it is no other than the whole mind which was in Christ Jesus."[20] And further, holiness is the goal because "without holiness no man shall see the Lord." Ultimately, in the New Birth we can be freed from sin toward holiness and wholeness, toward harmony with God and neighbor. When we come out as queer, we are freed from the expectation of heterosexuality and gender conformity, freed from a life of lying, of trying to fit a square peg in a round hole. And we are freed toward a right thinking of ourselves as children of God, in the image of God, toward a life of perfect love without fear. Coming out is a transformation. It results in seeing both ourselves and others anew and living in truly new ways that embody holiness and resist sin.

Marcella Althaus-Reid tells a story of a gay man she knew who finally came out after living for far too long a life that felt more like death. "He changed his name to 'Renato,'" she says, "which in Spanish means 'reborn' and he felt that it was his moment of resurrection from death."[21] Renato's coming out was a New Birth that even required a new name. His old life of sin—that is, of shame and pain and lies—had to die and he had to be born again into a new life of freedom and love and truth—that is, of holiness.

The New Birth does not guarantee a life without struggle. The Lord tells Cain that "sin is crouching at your door; it desires to devour you" (Gen 4:6) and Peter warns that "the devil prowls around like a lion looking for someone to devour" (1 Pet 5:8). Moving into what is new always requires the death of what is old. Further, the sin of heteronormativity and heterosexism does not go away once you come out. It is unrelenting. For many people, coming out is not a one-time event. It is a constant negotiation of surroundings, situations, and relationships that requires repentance and

19. Wesley, *Works* 2:193.
20. Wesley, *Works* 2:194.
21. Althaus-Reid, *Indecent Theology*, 123.

reassessment time and time again. But the rebirth, the resurrection, is always away from evil and into grace. What is ahead is always better than what is left behind.

Wesley insists that one cannot achieve the holiness required for salvation without the New Birth. He champions "the necessity of holiness in order to glory—and consequently of the New Birth, since none can be holy except he be born again."[22] The perfect love required to live a whole and healthy life cannot be achieved without coming out. To remain stewing in the sin of the closet is to deny the life of the New Birth and to stay captive to the state in which "every desire which is not according to the will of God is liable to 'pierce us through with many sorrows.'"[23] The life of the closet is sorrow and death, but God offers us so much more.

One common argument against LGBTQ+ inclusion in the church goes something like this: "Don't we believe in the transformative power of God? Don't we believe God can break chains and change lives?" When faced with these questions, my answer is always a resounding, "YES!" I absolutely believe in the grace of God that turns hopelessness and evil into joy and love and awakens a heart shrouded in death into new life. But this has little to nothing to do with sexuality, much less a movement from queerness to heterosexuality. In fact, it might indeed have more to do with the opposite movement.

Wesley says the reason we must be born again is that we are steeped in the human condition of sin. This is certainly true in the life of queer folks: born into a society where you are deemed an aberrance, a mutation, and told as much; where you are continually smothered with a narrative that strips you of your expression of the image of God. Such an existence will naturally do a number on your ability to love and be loved and express and experience holiness. But the grace of God tells a different story. It says that all people are made in God's image—capable of holiness and worthy of love as they are. And that narrative can make a transformative difference. It can breathe into the death that is dealt by heteropatriarchal structures the hope of new life, a life, Wesley says, that is "created anew in Christ Jesus" and "renewed after the image of God, in righteousness and holiness" toward the love of God. Said another way, the new life animated by Christ renews the image of God that has been damaged in queer people and enlivens the justice and love in the individual that are the marks of God's character.

22. Wesley, *Works* 2:195.

23. Wesley, *Works* 2:196. This quote references 1 Tim 6:10.

Wesley chides those who claim, "I constantly attend all ordinances of God: I keep to my church and sacrament," saying, "It is well you do. But all this will not keep you from hell, except you be born again."[24] The sins of the closet—the sins of heteronormativity, dishonesty, and shame—are not alleviated by church services, prayers, sermons, or books, Wesley says. One must be born again. One must come out, embracing the fullness of themselves and reclaiming the moral image of God in their lives, which is the image of perfect love that casts out fear.

Rather than be an agent of the degradation of LGBTQ+ life, forcing queers into the lonely and unlovely place of self-hate and self-harm, what if the church was a midwife in the ushering in of a New Birth of LGBTQ+ people, helping them to come out and embrace a life of love and righteousness, blessed by the grace of God?

24. Wesley, *Works* 2:200.

CIRCUMCISION OF THE HEART

To be circumcised in the first place could be considered, in some way, to be made queer. It is to alter a sexual organ to something other than "natural," and further to subscribe to a mode of being that is super-natural. It is an anti-normative act following an anti-normative code.

In the Hebrew Bible, circumcision is first introduced in Genesis 17. God says to Abraham, "This is my covenant, which you shall keep, between me and you and your offspring after you: Every male among you shall be circumcised" (Gen 17:10). The cutting of the foreskin of the males of Abraham's family was to be a sign of his covenant with God, which promised that Abraham would be "the ancestor of a multitude of nations" (Gen 17:4). If any male of this multitude of offspring (or any male brought into the family by purchase or other means) did not have his foreskin cut off, *he* would be cut off from the family, and therefore from God. Therefore, in demanding the practice of circumcision, God was perhaps creating a kind of queer community, marked by the difference of their genitals as belonging to each other and to God. In Joshua 4, Joshua has to circumcise all the male Israelites before they enter the Promised Land. All the circumcised Israelites who left Egypt had died in the forty intervening years, and the children born in the wilderness "had not been circumcised on the way" (Josh 4:7), and so before this peculiar people could enter their own land, they had to be circumcised to remind them of their queerness as the people of God who were receiving their promise. This material queerness was essential in constructing the Israelites' identity as the people of God.

Historically, circumcision has been a point of departure for anti-Semitism, deeply intertwined with misogyny. Daniel Boyarin explains that "the (male) Jewish body has been feminized: male Jews menstruate in the folklore of much of Europe, and circumcision has been repeatedly blamed

25

for the femaleness (weakness, passivity) of the Jew."[1] The transgender queerness of the menstruating circumcised male served as justification for the oppression of all Jews, simultaneously maligning people who were circumcised and people who menstruated as weak and non-normative, that is, not identifying with the ideal strong white Christian European man. This combination of stigma, placed on Jews by the dominant group, reminds us that the word "queer" itself is and has been used as a slur, and is only now being asserted positively in constructive moves of theory and community.[2] That which falls outside the hegemonic norms is denigrated and ridiculed into submission or extinction.[3] For Jews to hold on to circumcision—this queer mark—in the face of threat, harm, and ridicule is to assert a radical allegiance to a queer identity that is ultimately the specific grace and gifting of God. It is to embrace this God-given identity and follow God in God's promise to God's people, rather than submit to the powers that would have the Jewish people conform to "worldly" norms.

To circumcise the *heart*, then, is to further queer the practice. In the circumcision of the heart, circumcision becomes no longer restricted to and by gender and sex, but rather is made open to (or indeed required of) all who would follow God. The first instance of the circumcision of the heart in the Hebrew Bible is in Deuteronomy 10:

> Although heaven and the heaven of heavens belong to the LORD your God, the earth with all that is in it, yet the LORD set his heart in love on your ancestors alone and chose you, their descendants after them, out of all the peoples, as it is today. Circumcise, then, the foreskin of your heart, and do not be stubborn any longer. For the LORD your God is God of gods and Lord of lords, the great God, mighty and awesome, who is not partial and takes no bribe, who executes justice for the orphan and the widow, and who loves the strangers, providing them food and clothing. (Deut 10:14–18)

The passage talks about God's requirements of God's people, including fearing, serving, and loving God as well as caring for the stranger. None of these acts of devotion, of course, is restricted by genital configuration,

1. Boyarin, *Radical Jew*, 17.

2. Patrick Cheng explains that "the LGBT community has taken a word that was originally viewed as a highly offensive slur and transformed it into a positive description of the incredible diversity and transgressivity that is within the community." Cheng, *From Sin to Amazing Grace*, xvii.

3. Some extreme examples are the Shoah or the 1998 murder of Matthew Sheppard in Wyoming.

much less gender expression or sexual orientation. Indeed, people without a penis, without a physical foreskin, are said to have a foreskin of their hearts and are instructed to circumcise it. Loving God and loving others is the universal call for *all* of God's people, and this seems to be the result of a circumcised heart.

In Jeremiah 4, the prophet says:

> Circumcise yourselves to the LORD,
>   remove the foreskin of your hearts,
>   O people of Judah and inhabitants of Jerusalem,
> or else my wrath will go forth like fire,
>   and burn with no one to quench it,
>   because of the evil of your doings. (Jer 4:4)

Here it seems that to circumcise or remove the foreskin of one's heart is the opposite of, or the antidote to, "evil in your doings." The circumcision of the heart is what keeps God's people from God's wrath.

Further, while genital circumcision was a point of contention in early Christianity, whether followers of Jesus should be circumcised as Jews or not,[4] the spiritual, rather than material, "circumcision of the heart" is taken up as the mark of the Christian. Indeed, in the text Wesley focuses on in this sermon, Paul asserts against the Judaizers that "*real* circumcision is a matter of the heart" (Rom 2:29; emphasis mine), that the literal circumcision of the penis is actually inconsequential in the eyes of God. What God *really* cares about is not the state of one's genitals, but the state of one's heart. Whereas literal circumcision requires a penis—and specifically a biologically "normative" one, at that—the metaphorical circumcision of the heart is not limited to a certain genital configuration.

To circumcise the heart is similarly to be made queer in that, like genital circumcision, it is a resistance to normative powers and expectations.[5] Wesley says that "the circumcision of the heart, the seal of thy calling, is foolishness with the world,"[6] that is, it is *queer*. It is contrary to the world's normative expectations of how a life "should" be lived. Where one might be expected to be self-preserving and thrifty, God calls for God's people to provide for the poor and the widow and care for complete strangers.

---

4. See Paul's Letters to the Galatians and the Corinthians.

5. It is worth noting, if just briefly to bring up the question, that circumcision actually *is* the norm in the United States and has been for some time. What does it mean when the non-normative or non-"natural" becomes the norm?

6. Wesley, *Works* 1:402.

This selfless behavior is certainly contrary to the norms of the world—particularly the twenty-first century Western capitalist world—that prizes individual success and wealth above all else, and even sometimes contrary to our own desires for security and power. Just as the Jews' embrace of their circumcision is an embrace of a certain queerness, to embrace the circumcision of the heart that Wesley pulls from Scripture is to embrace a certain queerness. That queer, self-giving, justice-seeking life that Christians are called to, that we are marked by our hearts' circumcision for, is the life of holiness.

Above, I have established that we might characterize circumcision of the heart as queer. Additionally, Wesley asserts that circumcision of the heart is characterized as holiness. Therefore, perhaps holiness may also be considered queer.

Wesley's sermon consists of two parts: first, the question of the nature of the circumcision of the heart; second, some reflections on that nature. He concludes, in the first place, that circumcision of the heart, in general, is *holiness*, that is, the "habitual disposition of the soul . . . which implies being cleansed from sin . . . and endued with those virtues which were also in Christ Jesus."[7] This disposition and these virtues are not, as Wesley says, exhibited by any outward form, but by "a right state of soul, a mind and spirit renewed after the image of Him that created it."[8] In a queer paradigm, gender or sexuality may not be deduced simply by an "outward form," that is, say, genital configuration or personal appearance, and so similarly, for Wesley, holiness requires an examination of the state of the *heart*. While one may think it easy to deduce by another's outward form whether they've been cleansed from sin or whether their spirit has been renewed to be like Christ's, Wesley here insists to the contrary that holiness is rather a matter of the heart.

In particular, Wesley uses the second part of his sermon to assert that holiness has four markers: humility, faith, hope, and charity. These four markers might be surprising if one were to expect holiness to be marked by other characteristics of piety and purity, like submission, preservation, decency, or control. But these are not the markers Wesley sees or emphasizes. The markers of holiness that Wesley identifies are not in the static, austere, preservationist paradigm of holiness that fears contamination, but rather

---

7. Wesley, *Works* 1:402–3.
8. Wesley, *Works* 1:402.

markers of a queer paradigm of openness to all kinds of non-normative difference that transforms lives into queer Christlikeness.

Humility, faith, hope, and love can be markers of queerness as well as holiness, rendering Wesley's presentation of holiness as queer. Looking at how these markers of holiness find their expression in the lives and thought of LGBTQ+ Christians and theorists can help us problematize and reconstruct the ideas of humility, faith, hope, and love as they are presented in a restrictive heteronormative paradigm and expand how we understand them and what they might look like in practice. Let us now consider each of these markers and how they might be read as queer, thereby queering holiness itself.

Humility, at the first, is for Wesley "a right judgment of ourselves," particularly regarding "the sinfulness and helplessness of our nature."[9] For queer people, being told they are sinful and helpless is nothing new. Indeed, they have *been humbled* by church and society. In the normative hierarchy of cis-heteropatriarchy—that is, the structure of society in which cisgender, heterosexual men establish and maintain norms—the queer are firmly placed in the slots at the bottom, the slots of humility. In fact, we might say in being humbled queer people have actually had a *wrong* judgment of themselves imparted upon them.

Feminist theologian Valerie Saiving Goldstein suggests in her classic essay, "The Human Situation: A Feminine View," that the entire conception of sin in Western Christianity has been centered on male (and, we could add, heterosexual) experience, and in particular the experience of pride, which is why pride is considered to be at the core of sin.[10] She says that this male conception of sin is essentially pride in that it is characterized by "magnifying its own power, righteousness, or knowledge" and that "sin is the unjustified concern of the self for its own power and prestige."[11] However, Saiving Goldstein asserts, this male experience and conception of sin as pride is not the same as the feminine experience of sin. Further, she argues, if sin is something experienced by all people, its conception should be characterized by a *common* experience, not by the (straight, cisgender) male experience, which is different from the female (or homosexual, transgender, etc.) experience.

9. Wesley, *Works* 1:403.

10. Cf. Augustine, *City of God* XIV.13–14.

11. Goldstein, "Human Situation," 100.

The issue of pride and humility as the loci of sin and holiness, respectively, is then problematized—for men and women, and for people of other genders, as well as for people of various sexualities. If pride is *not* in fact an essential characteristic of sin in all people, we must rethink what role humility plays in a universalized conception of holiness. Goldstein's argument can be expanded from being primarily about women to the LGBTQ+ community as well. Just as pride is not the essential characteristic of feminine sin, according to Goldstein, perhaps neither is it the essential characteristic of LGBTQ+ sin. Cheng quotes Elizabeth Stuart's suggestion that "the 'sin' of LGBT people is not so much 'individual disobedience rooted in pride,' but rather 'not loving ourselves enough, of not having enough pride in ourselves.'"[12] Instead of the straight, cisgender male sin of pride that must be remedied with holy humility, the LGBTQ+ conception of sin might be a different kind of wrong judgment of self, which must be remedied by a kind of holy pride. If, as Wesley says, humility is having a "right judgment of oneself," for queer folk "humility," in the holiness sense, may actually look a lot like "pride."[13] Wesleyan churches may indeed have committed the sin of pride in judging themselves as better, more right, or more holy than LGBTQ+ people. To right this wrong may require the embrace of a queer holiness in which all people may judge themselves rightly as beloved creations of God struggling together for redemption and justice.

Wesley says that "the best guide of the blind . . . is faith."[14] It's telling here that the best guide of the blind is not *sight* or *light*, but *faith*. Holiness does not require us to be shaped into exemplars of normative "wholeness" determined by a hegemonic definition of what is right and good, but rather to yield to the guidance and provision of God, embracing our bodies, abilities, and identities in light of that faith. Resisting the demand for bodies to conform to this hegemonic ideal is queer. And here we see, it is also faithful.

Indeed, attaining this kind of singular ideal of wholeness and holiness in terms of gender and sexuality is impossible. For instance, in her book *Sex/Gender: Biology in a Social World*, Anne Fausto-Sterling says that "there are probably so many contributing streams [in the development of human embryos] and they probably interact in so many different ways, that

---

12. Cheng, *From Sin to Amazing Grace*, 114.

13. Elizabeth Edman argues exactly this in her book *Queer Virtue*, which I will discuss in the next section.

14. Wesley, *Works* 1:404.

we will never have a single story to tell about gender development."[15] The very development of humans and their genders and sexualities is queer. The complex contingencies of development resist norms at every turn. The faith of a queer holiness does not trust in a God who transforms people by a Stepford-like mold into models of perfect submission and docility, of heterosexuality and straight gender. Rather, the faith of queer holiness trusts in a God who creates in an infinite diversity, the Leviathan frolicking in the *tehom* and calling all God's creation *tov.* The chaotic abyss of the deep produces a creation that is good, acceptable, perfect, whole, in all its abundant anarchic variety.

In faith, there is risk—risk of difference and conflict and untamable passion—but risk is what makes faith real. Faith founded in certainty, sameness, and safety is no faith at all. Ethicist Mark Jordan identifies this un-faith of certainty as the "vice of the obligatory answer"—the assumption that there must be a rule for every question and Christian ethics must answer.[16] A so-called faith that champions and shelters norms and ideals rather than chasing after risk and encouraging creativity and exploration is beholden to this vice, not to the God witnessed to by the faith of queer holiness.

In fact, the vice of the obligatory answer values right-knowing so much that it covers over and smooths out any ambiguity or unevenness in tradition, Scripture, experience, or reason in order to create and subsequently adhere to a norm. For example, Jordan points out that the words "sodomy" and "homosexuality" are not themselves in the Bible (though some translators have rendered words as such), and that other words such as "fornication" and "adultery" actually conceal as much as they reveal.[17] To pretend to know all meanings and applications of Scripture while ignoring its complexity and ambiguity, and further to do so in a way that harms and marginalizes others, cannot be the work of holiness faith. A queer faith that is the surest guide of the blind is not a faith that trusts in the certainty and sureness of light or sight but in the risk-taking, creative, and all-loving God, the author of the gloriously uncertain, ambiguous, and queer creation.

15. Fausto-Sterling, *Sex/Gender*, 57.

16. Jordan, *Ethics of Sex*, 7.

17. Jordan, *Ethics of Sex*, 23. Jordan goes on to point out that churches tend to cite the Bible as if it is a coherent universal code. Besides the fact that it is not coherent or universal, most of the sexual prohibitions they point to in Leviticus, to condemn homosexuality for instance, are "part of a system of purity taboos that Christians have not observed." So to use the Bible in this prescriptive way is rather nonsensical.

Nazarene theologian Mildred Bangs Wynkoop says that "faith is not the boundary around the Christian which sets him apart and defines him. It is the 'growing edge' which keeps him from mere definition and makes him a flowing-out life, a dynamo of love."[18] Faith is not defining, then, in the sense that it makes the life of the Christian *definite*, but instead it is the point of departure from where the Christian might fling herself into the risk of life and love. Faith is the openness to the *infinite*. Faith is a transformative trust in all the various and mysterious actions of God. Therefore, inasmuch as this wide-open faith of holiness leads us in our blindness along a path toward loving God-knows-what, there is a very good chance that this faith is queer.

For Wesley, hope is the assurance of the Spirit that a person is indeed "in the path which leadeth to life," aided by God to persevere.[19] This hope and perseverance requires discipline, that is "daily care," to rid the heart of pollution. The pollution Wesley describes includes uncleanness, envy, malice, and wrath, passions and tempers that are "after the flesh."[20] Like humility, hope requires a right judgment of ourselves and our sin—an identification that it is couched in, and must be cut out of, the heart.

Sin, according to Wesley's sermon, is located in "passions and tempers [i.e., dispositions]"; thereby, opposite to such sin stands hope as an assurance of God's provision and help to do the work of purifying the heart. This is not a kind of spiritual calorie-counting to stay on the right track; rather, holiness hopes in God to will our purification against calculation. This becomes more telling when one notices that much of Wesley's discussion of discipline takes place in his discussion of hope.

For example, Wesley believes discipline must be intimately tied to hope, signaling that the discipline he believes is required for holiness is not based in a kind of will to power (which would be part of the sin of pride) but rather is based in the hope that God will do it, that God *is* doing it, that God's prevenient grace goes ahead of us and makes our way for holiness. Holiness hopes in God that the dispositions of our heart will ultimately be rooted not in evil but in love—perhaps any and all kind of love that moves us away from envy, malice, wrath, and uncleanness. Further, in a heteronormative paradigm, "uncleanness" may immediately signal some kind of (perhaps homo-)sexual impropriety, but when thinking queerly, we may

18. Wynkoop, *Theology of Love*, 248.
19. Wesley, *Works* 1:406.
20. Wesley, *Works* 1:407.

notice that its parallelism with envy, malice, and wrath—again, dispositions of the heart—makes it out to be perhaps something more like an unlovely way of thinking, or a desire driven by selfishness or greed. For all the airtime given to the Christian obsession with sexual sins, in the Bible and the tradition of the church, sexual sins have only been one aspect—indeed, a small one—of what is considered sin.

Thinking of LGBTQ+ issues specifically, Cheng points out that of more than 31,000 verses in the Bible, the church has focused in on just six to construct their beliefs about homosexuality.[21] Therefore to assume "uncleanness" would refer solely or primarily to sexual sin—and homosexuality, at that—is grossly misguided. The hope of holiness is in a broader, more holistic wholeness that brings the whole person into perfect love, in all aspects of life, not hung up on genital acts alone. And further, because of Wesley's, and the Bible's, emphasis on the state of the heart as the progenitor of sin or love, we might conclude that holiness is not about the genital acts at all, but rather the intent behind and consequences subsequent to those acts. Therefore, certainly some queer sex or relationships might be sinful, unclean, unlovely, driven by selfishness or greed, just as some heterosexual sex or relationships might be. But, as Wendy Farley points out, "there is no call for heterosexual men to deny their sexuality altogether because some of them use it badly."[22] The persevering discipline in hope that Wesley is calling for in this sermon is a discipline toward a holistic holiness that is centered on love—inclusive of the whole person and their acts and, primarily, dispositions, that they would be characterized by love rather than evil.

We might also question what "uncleanness" and "cleanness" really are in the first place, and how these distinctions might become muddied in the life of Jesus, who ate with sinners and prostitutes, or in the stories Jesus tells, like the ritually "clean" Levite who left the injured man in the ditch while the "unclean" Samaritan helped him. Perhaps the circumcision of the heart is not as clean a cut as we might think.

Later in the sermon, Wesley briefly identifies hope with joy.[23] The assurance granted by hope frees people from the fear of risk, if not the uncertainty. It liberates people to take the risk of faith with abandon. There is certainly little structure or regimen or will-to-power in outright joy. One

21. Cheng, *From Sin to Amazing Grace*, 17.

22. Farley, *Gathering Those Driven Away*, 3.

23. Wesley, *Works* 1:411.

of the most common biblical examples of joy is David dancing before the Lord, shamelessly uncovering himself—very queer indeed.

Finally, Wesley adds as the crowning marker of the circumcision of the heart charity, or love. Love, he says, "is all the commandments in one," and that in love, ultimately, is perfection and holiness. He, of course, cites what he calls the "royal law of heaven and earth," that "Thou shalt love the Lord thy God with all thy heart, and with all thy soul, and with all thy mind, and with all thy strength," but he is quick to point out that (1) this does not forbid us to love anything other than God, in fact it implies that we *do* love others, and (2) it does not forbid us to take pleasure in anything other than God.[24] Therefore it's clear for Wesley that any true, unselfish love and pleasure that points to God is wrapped up in holiness. Indeed, this is a radical affirmation of all love and pleasure, perhaps even queer love and pleasure, inasmuch as it leads to God. Christine Gudorf argues that pleasure is itself a "premoral good," that is, though it does not necessarily lead to moral good, it is "ordinarily a good, and should be understood as one aspect of the general social good."[25] She discusses mutual sexual pleasure, especially, as a stage where we act out the injunction to love our neighbor as ourselves. She says that Christians often assume that loving the neighbor entails a denial of self, however, "sex is perhaps one of the best life arenas for demonstrating that self and other are not naturally hostile," and that "the interests of the self and the interests of the partner are largely linked."[26] Therefore, in the engagement of sexual pleasure, we very clearly love our neighbor as we love ourselves, thereby obeying God's law and demonstrating our love of God as well. In this way, any mutual sexual pleasure rooted in love can be a vital part of holiness. If love is the clearest and most important indicator of holiness, then surely we would do well to read "love" as inclusive of all the various kinds of love found in all the various kinds of relationships experienced between people—romantic and sexual, sure, even gay, lesbian, bisexual, pansexual, or polyamorous, and also platonic, parental, filial, asexual, erotic, temporary, enduring, and existing in the multitude of contours and expressions we see in our world. To limit what counts as love would be to put a limit on holiness, even the holiness of God, who has no limits.

---

24. Wesley, *Works* 1:407–8.

25. Gudorf, *Body, Sex, and Pleasure*, 90.

26. Gudorf, *Body, Sex, and Pleasure*, 94.

If circumcision of the heart is marked by humility, faith, hope, and charity, how might we think about such circumcision ecclesially? What does such a queer circumcision marked by a queered understanding of humility, faith, hope, and love look like in the church?

Perhaps the church might be circumcised by humility, such that we acknowledge that our place is not the seat of judgment whence we might demand adherence to some standard morality and behavior of questionable provenance. If the queer are already the humble, by virtue of their marginalization, perhaps the call for humility in the call for holiness is directed at the heteronormative *status quo* of the church, in which we need to identify our own "corrupt nature," that "confusion and ignorance and error reign over our understanding," and that perhaps the church itself needs to cleanse its mind "from those high conceits of our own perfection,"[27] acknowledging that the grace and love of God should be the chief dictate of our behavior and relationships, not a heteropatriarchal hierarchy. Indeed, the church might learn from those queer people it has marginalized how to have a "right judgment of ourselves," that is, not only to identify and acknowledge our propensity for sin and infirmity, but also to embrace the inalienable *imago dei* in all of humanity. In Elizabeth Edman's book, *Queer Virtue*, she identifies queer pride as one of the virtues embodied by the LGBTQ+ community that the church would do well to emulate. She asserts that "Pride begins first and foremost with the ability to see oneself."[28] In other words, we might say that pride is "a right judgment of ourselves," which is exactly how Wesley defines humility. A reversal of pride and humility may be in order to achieve a queer holiness in a queer church. Edman goes on to say that "defining sin as pride, as hubris, may be appropriate for people of privilege . . . but for those who have been colonized, dehumanized, demonized," it can "extend and exacerbate oppression."[29] Such a reversal is entirely consistent with, indeed emblematic of, the Kingdom of God, in which the exalted are humbled and the humbled exalted. Therefore, the least our churches can do is include our queer friends, the least of these, in our congregations and our leadership.

Perhaps the church might be circumcised by faith, such that we come to rely not on our own sight, following the path we see as right in our own eyes, but rather on the provision of the gracious God, who leads us in the

---

27. Wesley, *Works* 1:411.

28. Edman, *Queer Virtue*, 109.

29. Edman, *Queer Virtue*, 115.

way of righteousness and love. To inhabit spaces of normative privilege (to be, for the sake of the metaphor, "sighted") is, indeed, only to see in part. The eyes of faith are those that "pull down strongholds," "overturn all prejudices of corrupt reason," "cast down every high thing that exalteth itself against the knowledge of God."[30] The eyes of faith are not the eyes of the normative powers, they are the queer eyes that see as Christ sees. To look on others with the queer eyes of faith is to look toward mutual liberation. It is to disrupt the systems that exclude and reject and place themselves as the ultimate authority and rule rather than God. The eyes of faith direct our touching, tasting queer blindness toward God's love, which does not restore our sight, but transforms it. A church marked by queer faith embraces people as they are, trusting that the God who made them, who loves them, is faithful to work in them as God will. A church marked by queer faith embodies the belief of the church mothers cooing over the newest tiny congregant, that "God don't make no junk." God knows what God is doing, even when what God is doing seems queer beyond our reckoning. A church marked by queer faith takes all the risks required by a true hospitality to the other, a true love and acceptance of the neighbor and the stranger alike.

Perhaps the church might be circumcised by hope in which we have joyful assurance of God doing God's work in all hearts to rid them of evil and fill them with love. This hope manifests as joy in the divine fulfillment of holiness in us, not as anxiety rooted in achieving some purity of our own design and effort. So perhaps this hope looks like denying the impulse to require adherence to a strict code of conduct, but rather abiding in the queer hope that God works in hearts in an abundant diversity of ways, all leading toward Christian perfection, freedom, and holiness. A denial of a legalistic dependence on codes frees us to take responsibility for our own spiritual discipline. It requires us to practice conforming our lives to the perfect love of God and neighbor, and to wrestle with what that means in our lives individually and ecclesially. The discipline of learning to love is messy when there are no facile rules to fall back on, but yet we have hope that God is in that mess with us, guiding us in and toward the love God has commanded of us. In the discipline of queer hope, there is no striving but rest. Rather than looking for some future glory, for some unattainable perfection in the distance, queer hope brings that glory into the present and says that perfection of love can be ours now—a thoroughly Wesleyan teaching. As we sing in the Fanny Crosby hymn, "Blessed Assurance":

30. Wesley, *Works* 1:404–5.

Perfect submission, perfect delight!
Visions of rapture now burst on my sight;
Angels descending bring from above
Echoes of mercy, whispers of love.[31]

A church marked by queer hope leans into the joyful assurance that God is working now to transform our hearts from progenitors of evil dispositions to founts of perfect love, and that the discipline this requires is not about acting "good" or morally respectable so that we may receive mercy and love in the future, but hoping in and receiving the work God is doing in all people here and now.

And perhaps the church might be circumcised by love, wherein love and affection—toward any and all others—as well as all manner of pleasure might contribute to and bolster our holiness, inasmuch as it leads us to love the One who is the Creator of such love and pleasure. That is, rather than hide from, reject, or proscribe queer varieties of love, the church might embrace them as equal and valid conduits of loving God. Holiness churches have been afraid of pleasure for too long, fearing that it somehow contradicts Wesley's (and by extension, God's) calls for humility and self-denial. But Wesley makes it very clear in this sermon that pleasure should not be completely rejected as sinful, but can indeed lead us to God. A queer embrace of pleasure as a byproduct of love is an essential mark of holiness, and holiness churches would do well to open themselves to this aspect of it rather than shutting themselves off from it. True and unselfish love—and its byproduct, pleasure—is always a mark of holiness; therefore, if churches reject queer love they incidentally reject a Wesleyan understanding of holiness in the process. To condemn queer pleasure and queer love is not to champion holiness, but to deny it.

If Kierkegaard identified holiness as purity of the heart, that is to will one thing, we might say that Wesley identifies holiness as circumcision of the heart, to will queer things. Inasmuch as circumcision of the heart is queer, holiness is queer, and we can read Wesley's understanding of holiness as urging us toward a love as expansive and unlimited as God's love in Christ. The markers of the circumcision of the heart that Wesley recognizes as holiness—humility, faith, hope, and love—all might point together toward a rather queer existence. If humility is right judgment of ourselves, it might actually look more like Elizabeth Edman's queer pride, and it might call the church's heteronormative powers to account and to repent. Faith

---

31. Crosby, "Blessed Assurance," 369.

revels in the risk and uncertainty of God's queer creation and calls the church to see this creation with queer eyes that trust in God rather than our own supposed sight. Queer hope rethinks what discipline looks like in holiness, grounding it on the hope of what God does in our lives rather than how "good" we can be, and calls the church to embrace the joy of God's provision and transformation of hearts here and now rather than forcing people to conform to an untenable, constantly deferred moral ideal. Love is the ultimate marker of holiness, and queer love—as well as pleasure—is as much an expression of holiness as any heterosexual love. Queer love challenges the church to practice what it preaches and truly embrace all people and all loves as emblematic of the holiness that they display. Holiness is ultimately the marker of Christian life—a life that declares the inbreaking of the queer Kingdom of God in which the mighty are cast down, the rich are sent away, and the exalted are humbled, in which, perhaps, the normative have received their reward, but the queer shall be abundantly blessed.

ON PERFECTION

In his sermon "On Perfection," John Wesley endeavors to make his case about the role of perfection in the life of the Christian and how it is possible, indeed commanded of Christians, despite others' arguments to the contrary. Written in 1784, this sermon serves as a concise yet comprehensive demonstration of Wesley's understanding of the most central theme of his work. There is no treatment or grasp of Wesley without a treatment or grasp of Christian perfection and holiness. This sermon in particular reveals how Wesley had concluded that "the whole question boiled down to two issues: (1) the definition of 'perfection' in terms of a Christian's love of God and neighbor—no less but also no more; and (2) the definition of sin as deliberate."[1] These two framing issues serve us well in understanding Wesleyan holiness and Christian perfection in general, but also for cultivating a queer understanding of holiness and perfection. Just as, in the context of this sermon and its delivery, Wesley encountered people who denied the possibility of a person attaining any measure of perfection, many people today deny the possibility of LGBTQ+ persons being Christian, much less attaining perfection in their own right.

Wesley's sermon consists of three parts: to show what perfection is; to answer some objections to it; and to expostulate a little with the opponents of it. In this chapter, we will follow the same structure, but instead of thinking about perfection generally as Wesley does, we will apply his same argument to the perfection achievable by LGBTQ+ persons specifically, given their particular experiences, concerns, challenges, and opponents.

First, what does perfection look like to Wesley, and what does it look like in the lives of LGBTQ+ people? Wesley makes an important distinction

---

1. Editor Albert Outler's introductory commentary to the sermon in Wesley, *Works* 3:70–71.

about what *kind* of perfection he is talking about, so as to be clear that such a state is indeed attainable. It is not "Adamic perfection" or "angelic perfection," but rather perfection "under the law of love." Wesley agrees that it is impossible for a person to achieve Adamic or angelic perfection, that is, perfection such as was enjoyed by the prelapsarian first human, or the angels, who have a lesser capacity for corruptibility than humanity. Even having attained Christian perfection, a person is not immune to "ignorance, and error, and a thousand other infirmities."[2] Mistakes and ignorances are part and parcel of humanity, but they are not impediments to perfection. Because for Wesley perfection is about complete orientation to love, and not a teleological functional rightness, one can be understood to have attained Christian perfection while still experiencing "infirmities" or committing mistakes out of ignorance. "This is the sum of Christian perfection," Wesley says. "It is all comprised in that one word, love."[3] Love is at the center of any scriptural or traditional account of perfection: having the mind of Christ, abiding by the Greatest Commandments, manifesting of the fruit of the Spirit, renewing the image of God in the person. Wesley cites several biblical references to holiness and perfection, and he shows that they all point back to perfect love. Further, Wesley draws the equivalence between perfection, that is, perfect love, and salvation. To be saved is, in part, to be saved from sin; to be saved from sin is to be made perfect; and to be made perfect is to be made perfect in love. Ultimately, to believe that one can be saved by Christ through the Spirit is to believe one can be made perfect in love.

The terms and concepts of perfection and sanctification take on different meanings in different contexts and for different people within the Wesleyan tradition. Some separate them out, in order to solve the question of process or crisis—they say perfection is the process a Christian pursues and hones, and sanctification is finally achieved or granted in the moment of crisis. Others equate the two entirely, either claiming that both occur in a moment or that both are a matter of gradual growth. Either way, for Wesley, the point is that sinless perfection was a real possibility for Christians in this life. Mildred Bangs Wynkoop claims that Wesley's "deepest conviction was that man could be saved from sin here on this earth and in this life and live in the atmosphere of love to God and man."[4] It was a practical concern,

2. Wesley, *Works* 3:73.
3. Wesley, *Works* 3:74.
4. Wynkoop, *Theology of Love*, 270.

a joining of the traditional theological doctrines of the church with the subjective experience of people's everyday lives.

Wesley's definition of perfection, based on his reading of Scripture, is "pure love filling the heart, and governing all the words and actions."[5] To be motivated always and only by love above all defies the hegemonic structures of our world. The binaries, norms, and restrictions that govern our Western culture in particular, specifically with regard to gender and sexuality and their assumptions and implications, are set up in service of patriarchal domination, capitalist rule, and racist oppression. The chief motivations that perpetuate these societal systems are fear and greed. To act from a heart filled with love, that is, true concern and care for others, whom we see and know to be valuable simply for their common existence, will always work against the normative powers. Queer love in particular challenges these unjust structures because it is doubly resistant. Unproductive,[6] unafraid, unfazed by the restrictive demands of how, for example, romantic relationships should work for the reproduction of our oppressive society, queer love lets *love* make the calls, and so embodies the *ethos* of Wesleyan perfection.

"Perfection," to Wesley, Wynkoop says, "was to be defined rationally, biblically, ethically, socially."[7] It is apparent chiefly in relationship, revealed in right treatment of others, witnessed to in the Scriptures, and consistent with reason. It is not to be found in a personal pietism, but rather, because its basis is love, perfection is necessarily toward the other. Perfection acts up and acts out. The person who has been cleansed of sin and filled with perfect love will ever be working toward justice, which upends the normative systems of evil that dampen, obscure, and otherwise negate the primacy of love in the world.

The implications for Wesleyan perfection as perfect love are so much broader than a conceptualization of perfection as an individualized piety or keeping of rules. Wynkoop insists that perfection is *not* a moral

---

5. Wesley, *Works* 11:401; Wynkoop, *Theology of Love*, 272.

6. I mean "unproductive" in both the literal reproductive sense, that gay men and lesbians tend not to physically conceive and birth children, but also in the sense that non-normative relationships refuse the reproduction of structures such as marriage, with its subservience and complicity to capitalist norms and governmental restrictions that are often narrativized as "benefits" but that in fact perpetuate various types of gender, race, and economic oppression. For more on this, see Spade and Willse, "Marriage Will Never Set Us Free."

7. Wynkoop, *Theology of Love*, 273.

perfection*ism*. "Perfectionism," she says, "substitutes external and amoral demonstration for inward grace."[8] It is not a moralism defined by rules or piety, but rather an orientation of the heart, provided by grace, toward love. This orientation then manifests outwardly in ethical acts, right relationship with neighbor, and a devotion to God and God's rule of love for the world. This focus on orientation is worth noting, because in some Wesleyan circles where homosexuality is considered a sin, it is *not* the orientation that matters but rather the act. That is, one could *be* gay in orientation, and not sin, but only once one engages in "homosexual activity" (which is always unclear—is it holding hands? Kissing? Sex?) is one sinning. For Wesley, however, the intention is the key. The action is the outpouring of the intention, and it's either all sin or all not. If, having been cleansed from sin by the Spirit, the orientation of one's heart is toward love, and one's action is the outpouring of this love, then there can be no sin here.

Thinking perfection in terms of love brings it from the ethereal impossibility portrayed in other traditions into the reality of actual life, able to be experienced by actual people. Wesley's Christian perfection has practical implications both on the larger scale and personal levels, and they are all based on concrete experience. Wynkoop explains that "it was precisely that Christianity tended in his day to disregard the implications of Christian living now that urged him on to delineate holiness as love—practical, real, here and now."[9] Because of the practical here-ness of love that must be worked out in the messy mundane of real life and actual relationships, there are no hard and fast rules for getting to or living out perfection. It is relative and looks different for everyone. Just as love does not just look one way or manifest as one thing, perfection is multivalent and unpredictable. We are made holy by the wild and wily love of the Spirit, which cannot be controlled, defined, or contained. And so perfection, just as love, will do and look and be as it wills.

The first objection that Wesley brings up is that there is no indication in Scripture that Christian perfection can be achieved. He readily addresses this by providing several passages from both the Old and New Testaments to the effect that God promises our salvation and thereby our perfection, specifically in love. For example, he claims that "'Thou shalt love the Lord thy God with all thy heart, and with all thy soul, and with all thy mind,' [and] 'Thou shalt love thy neighbour as thyself,' is as express a promise as a

---

8. Wynkoop, *Theology of Love*, 281.

9. Wynkoop, *Theology of Love*, 298.

command."[10] The implication is that God would not command something of us that is not possible, therefore, if God commands and indeed requires perfection from us, then God also promises to make it a reality. God would not "mock his helpless creatures, calling us to receive what he never intends to give."[11] Therefore, Wesley concludes that God "turns all the commands into promises," and likewise then a command "is equivalent to a promise."[12] So all the biblical commands—particularly, in this case, the command to perfection—are possible for us to achieve.

Another objection Wesley raises is the objection that it is impossible to be sinless while a person is "in a sinful body."[13] Wesley concedes that Adamic perfection is not possible, for "while we are in the body we cannot be wholly free from mistake," and we are still "liable to judge wrong in many instances."[14] However, the mistakes and infirmities that are part of the condition of a post-fall humanity are not to be considered sins properly so-called, for they are not willful transgressions of a known law, that is, the law of love. To be mistaken in judgment cannot be said to be sinful or unloving in the same way as proper sins.

Further, Wesley rejects that a body can be sinful at all. "No body," he says, "or matter of any kind, can be sinful."[15] Sin does not reside in the material stuff of creation, but rather in the spiritual. Sin is not in the heart that beats but in the soul; it is not in the brain but in the mind. So because the body is not inherently sinful, or sinful in itself at all, it does not preclude a person's capacity for sinlessness.

This is an important point, particularly for post-enlightenment Western Protestant evangelical traditions within the Wesleyan scope. A distrust and ultimate negation and denigration of the body crept into the Christian imagination over time, but it has taken especially strong root in evangelicalism, with its emphasis on personal purity and piety. Set over against the mind or the spirit, the body has been seen as the source of sinful passions requiring chastening and control. With help from certain traditions of interpretation of the Apostle Paul and Saint Augustine, the body became not the site of the image of God in humanity but rather the site of

10. Wesley, *Works* 3:76–77.
11. Wesley, *Works* 3:77.
12. Wesley, *Works* 3:77.
13. Wesley, *Works* 3:79.
14. Wesley, *Works* 3:79.
15. Wesley, *Works* 3:80.

sinfulness. "Flesh and blood cannot inherit the kingdom of God" (1 Cor 15:50), for example, and the Augustinian emblem of concupiscence is the uncontrollability of an erection. The vilification of the body went hand in hand, then, with the heightened focus on sexual sin. The Protestant pre-occupation with bodies, sex, and sexuality has become more apparent in the wake of increasing visibility and awareness (as well as acceptance and inclusion) of LGBTQ+ persons. The evangelical reaction to homosexuality and transgender issues betrays a deep-seated rejection of engagement and attunement to bodily desires and interactions, and the high value placed on self-denial and austerity. Wesleyan evangelicals have appropriated Wesley to this end. With his interest and emphasis on rigorous self-examination and restraint in the service of pursuing holiness, Wesley seems an appropriate tool. However, to focus on Wesley's *methodism* over his exaltation of love over all else is a mistake. His pietism is always geared toward the social and embodied end of perfect love. It is not a legalism or "works-based salvation," but rather the practice of living into a holy life. And this holy life is not precluded by living in a body.

The body is not sinful, Wesley insists, and yet even if it were, "no more can these walls of flesh and blood hinder [God] a moment from sanctifying you throughout. He can just as easily save you from all sin in the body as out of the body."[16] If we believe in God's ability to move in us and in the world, then the fact of our being embodied will have no effect on God's work. Or rather, we will find that our embodiment is precisely what mediates God's work in our lives and in the world.

By labeling LGBTQ+ bodies primarily by their sexual proclivities or activities rather than by the indwelling of the image of God within them, queer bodies are wrongfully marked as inherently sinful. Pamela Lightsey says that "only when we can imagine our bodies fashioned as good rather than only in terms of sexual acts will we be able to usher in a healthy discussion on the sacred worth of queer bodies."[17] The Protestant preoccupation with sex has had broad implications for all people—heterosexual cisgender persons are also often labeled primarily in terms of sex even insofar as they are the "default"—and so such hangups regarding the sinfulness of the body will limit everyone's capacity for embracing holiness. And those who "deviate" from the norm will feel the negative effects most acutely and suffer for it. This is why queer liberation is truly liberation for all: if everyone is

---

16. Wesley, *Works* 3:80.
17. Lightsey, *Our Lives Matter*, 85.

suffering under the original sin of the forced strictures of heteronormitiv-
ity, then the policing of those brave enough to resist it lends power to those
who conform to sin and punishes those who attempt to free themselves
into wholeness and holiness. On the other hand, to undo these systems
that harm some and privilege others benefits everyone. Just as serving a
vegetarian meal satisfies both meat-eaters and not, or as installing a ramp
allows access to wheelchair users and not, creating a socially just world allows freedom for all. Creating a sexually liberated world allows liberty and
authenticity and self-determination for everyone.

A third objection Wesley addresses is the skepticism of perfection
given the apparent lack of witnesses or people who claim to have attained
it. If elimination of sin and a life of perfect love is possible, they wonder,
then where are these people? If it is so difficult or so rare as to never be
demonstrated, is it even worth claiming? Wesley concedes that there are
not very many examples of those who have attained Christian perfection,
particularly those who continue in it for long periods of time or until the
end of their lives. However, this fact does not keep him from asserting its
possibility. Wesley points out that some people may have experienced a
short period of time of perfection and then fallen back into sin by a sud-
den wrong choice or loss of faith. Wesley also emphasizes that what people
expect from Christian perfection is often too much, beyond its actual
definition and scope, and so of course they have not encountered a person
who is free from every sin *and* infirmity or mistake. But Wesley insists that
because sinless perfection is promised, it is possible, and though perhaps
the proof or examples are few, the goal is still worthwhile and the grace to
that end is abundant.

Wesley's answer to the objectors against Christian perfection is
couched in a certain naïve optimism. "Why should you be so averse to holiness?" he asks.[18] The objectors are skeptical and want proofs and details
about how such salvation could be, but Wesley's response is something like
a faithful, "Why not?" Why would anyone be "either afraid of, or averse to,
salvation from all sin?"[19] If it is commanded—and therefore promised—by
God, and it can reasonably be accepted as a desirable end for the Christian
life, then what reason is there to resist or deny it? Why do they so desire to

18. Wesley, *Works* 3:83.
19. Wesley, *Works* 3:83.

hold on to sin? As Wesley says, "Why are you so fond of sin? What good has it ever done you?"[20]

Similarly, there are people who would deny or reject LGBTQ+ people's inclusion in the church, their ability to be true Christians, or certainly their capacity for holiness. And perhaps the question is the same: Why should they be so averse to holiness? Why should holiness not manifest in LGBTQ+ people just as readily as in straight cisgender folks? What are they afraid of? Why would they not allow these brothers, sisters, and friends holiness? If Christian perfection and holiness are a result of the movement of the Spirit and the instantiation of perfect love, why would they want to deny this to LGBTQ+ people? Why would they restrict the movement of the Spirit or resist the appearance of love in the world? Surely a Christian, who believes in the grace of God and the promise of holiness and love, would wish for as many people as possible to experience and participate in this sanctified life.

Elizabeth Edman writes about the queer virtue of risk—the risks queer people take in coming out, in simply being themselves in the world, in challenging the norms of heteronormative society. She says that "risk is what happens when you have something that you value and you take a chance with it, hoping to achieve something of greater value," and that "identity-based risks involve putting on the line something that is part of you, hoping to get a return on that investment that will also be part of you."[21] Perhaps for the church, giving up the gatekeeping of holiness and the holding on to sin is a risk. Letting go of a traditional understanding and regulation of salvation involves a loss of control that many in the church are not eager to make. However, the reward for doing so is so much greater than the complacent comfort of control. The reward is the fresh, sweeping, generative rush of the Spirit. A revival, we might say. The inclusion of God's LGBTQ+ children in the enlivening work of God, or more rightly, the recognition of the Spirit's work in love that is already being done among queer folks, is an invigorating possibility far greater than the stagnant judgment of the misguided monotony of safe, scared sameness.

Wesley asks, "What are you afraid of?" What's the worst that could happen? What is there to lose? The embrace of queer perspectives and queer experiences in the Christian life and understanding of holiness opens up an expansive horizon of opportunity for God to do a new thing. By loosening

---

20. Wesley, Works 3:86.

21. Edman, Queer Virtue, 44.

the church's grip on restrictive binaries of sex, gender, and sexuality, we can avail ourselves of the limitless transformative power of God's love. As the saying goes, nothing changes if nothing changes. Action is necessary. A risk must be taken.

An insistence on justice leading to revival is part of the Wesleyan DNA. The initial Methodist revival in the Church of England precipitated by John Wesley himself was begun in no small part because of Wesley's commitment to caring for the poor and bettering the lives of laborers in the newly industrialized society. The revival of the Free Methodists led to their exclusion from the Methodist Episcopal Church because of their advocacy for justice on behalf of the poor and enslaved in the United States. At the 2019 General Conference of the United Methodist Church, the gathered delegates voted down plans for explicit inclusion and affirmation of LG-BTQ+ members and clergy in support of a more "traditional" plan that many felt denied the core Methodist claim of the sacred worth of all people. In the immediate aftermath of the vote, queer clergy and laity and other allies and advocates gathered in the entry hall of the convention center, singing hymns, marching, and partaking in eucharist in a spontaneous act of holy resistance where the Spirit was clearly present and at work. The joined hands, raised voices, and tear-stained faces of God's children who felt they had been denied their place in God's family despite their call, their faithfulness, and their work evoked the power of holy love in a way that the church is utterly foolish to dismiss and reject.

To deny LGBTQ+ people their place in the church, their position as clergy, or their own journey of holiness stands in opposition to so much of John Wesley's thought and the tradition of the Wesleyan denominations. The life of holiness demands one thing: perfect love. There is no reason that LGBTQ+ people would be refused this work of the Spirit in their lives, and in fact, in some ways their lives are prime spaces for such work. The experiences of queer people can lend themselves to an understanding of love that is as expansive and open, as far-reaching and uninhibited as the love of God itself. Perhaps it is the cleansing from the original sin of heteronormativity that our church needs in order for it to embrace this queer love and live into the holiness promised to us.

FREE GRACE

In addition to the well-known doctrine of holiness, another key compo-
nent of Wesley's theology is his insistence on free grace against predestination. Influenced by the Moravians, Wesley was a staunch Arminian and
was convinced that the Calvinist doctrine of predestination was contrary
to Scripture properly interpreted. His well-known personal and theological
dispute with his longtime frenemy George Whitefield resulted in a series of
intensely polemic writings against the Calvinist doctrine.

The purpose of this chapter is not necessarily to argue about predestination itself, or its potential for queerness—there are certainly queer
Calvinist theologies—but to approach this emblematically Wesleyan perspective from a queer angle. What can a queer reading of Wesley's insistence on agency in response to free grace offer as we construct a queer
Wesleyan theology?

Wesley's 1739 published sermon "Free Grace" was the first major blow
in what became a significant conflict. It states in no uncertain terms what
Wesley thinks about predestination and the people who preach it—that they
are cruel blasphemers and on the side of the devil. Albert Outler suggests
in his introduction to this sermon that it may not be the most accurate or
charitable description of Calvinist thought, but nevertheless it is "a useful
illustration of Wesley's temper and methods as a polemicist."[1] Despite his
love for Whitefield as a fellow laborer in Christ, Wesley's dogged rejection
of predestination drove him to speak harshly on this matter to his friend
and those who followed him.

Both Wesley and Whitefield were born and bred Anglicans, educated
and ordained in the Church of England and loyal to it throughout their
calls for its reformation. Their shared passion for revival resulted in their

---

1. Wesley, Works 3:543.

shared success in evangelism on both sides of the Atlantic, and their shared, though divergent, influence has echoed in Protestantism through the centuries. Their mutual influence of each other—Wesley in the role of older mentor and Whitefield in converting Wesley to an appreciation of outdoor field preaching, for example—made each of them into the iconic churchman he was. In this way, there truly could have been no Wesley without a Whitefield, and vice versa. Indeed, Whitefield's emphasis on evangelism and Wesley's focus on cultivating communities of accountability combined to deliver a one-two punch that developed the faith of hundreds across England and in the American colonies. However, they had deep and irreconcilable differences in their understandings of grace, salvation, and Christian perfection. At the root of these disagreements was the foundational disparity in their theologies: Whitefield's belief in the Calvinist doctrine of predestined election versus Wesley's claim of the Arminian doctrine of active response to free grace.

Nazarene Wesley scholar David McEwan explains that Wesley's conviction of the necessity of freedom for authentic love in response to God and neighbor was "at the heart of Wesley's rejection of the Reformed understanding of predestination and election," and one of the core issues in his disagreements with Whitefield.[2] For Wesley, McEwan continues, "a love that is compelled through original design, or by simple coercion from a greater power, would not be love at all."[3] Wesley's emphasis on relationship in his soteriology requires a focus on love, which is *enabled* by God through prevenient grace, but is not *forced* or *compelled* by God.

The first and most important point Wesley makes is that "the grace or love of God, whence cometh our salvation, is free in all, and free for all."[4] Contrary to common critiques of Arminian theology that say its denial of predestination means leaning too heavily on the works of individuals and not on the work of God, Wesley is insistent that God's grace and its resultant salvation is not dependent on human effort at all, but is completely a gift from God. God is the author and provider of all good things, and so, Wesley reasons, people's "good tempers, or good desires, or good purposes and intentions" are "the streams only, not the fountain. They are the fruits of free grace, and not the root."[5] Humanity does not generate our

2. McEwan, "I Am Yet Persuaded, You Do Greatly Err," 91.
3. McEwan, "I Am Yet Persuaded, You Do Greatly Err," 91.
4. Wesley, *Works* 3:544.
5. Wesley, *Works* 3:545.

own salvation, then, but we do respond to that salvation that is offered by God—freely and to all people.

Wesley's next concern is that predestination means that the gift of salvation is not truly offered to *all* people, but only to the elect, a belief he finds to be not only repugnant but inconsistent with the Bible and the character of a God of love. Wesley summarizes the belief thus: "By virtue of an eternal, unchangeable, irresistible decree of God, one part of mankind are infallibly saved, and the rest infallibly damned; it being impossible that any of the former should be damned, or that any of the latter should be saved."[6] While some of his opponents appear to argue for election to grace only, and not reprobation, Wesley demonstrates that one cannot contend for the former without the latter.

Since those who will be saved are elect from the beginning of the world and regardless of their own deeds, Wesley then concludes that therefore preaching or any evangelism would be irrelevant. "It is needless to them that are elected," he says, "for they, whether with preaching or without, will infallibly be saved," and it is also "useless to them that are not elected, for they cannot possibly be saved."[7] Why, Wesley asks, would God command Christians to preach, to spread the good news of the gospel, if it made no difference? Those who will be saved will be saved; those who will not, will not. No repentance, no change, no belief is required. So what good is preaching?

Further, Wesley says the doctrine of predestination tends to "destroy several particular branches of holiness," especially love of enemies.[8] He says believing that some people are inherently reprobate "naturally inspires contempt or coldness toward those whom we suppose outcasts from God."[9] That anyone would be treated as, much less truly *be*, outcast from God is unconscionable to Wesley. And he thinks it's unavoidable that believing certain people "to have been hated of God from eternity" would lead one also to hate them.[10] The finality and certainty of predestination left no reason, in Wesley's view, for love of one's neighbor, whose fate was already determined as well as one's own.

6. Wesley, *Works* 3:547.

7. Wesley, *Works* 3:547.

8. Wesley, *Works* 3:548.

9. Wesley, *Works* 3:548.

10. Wesley, *Works* 3:549.

Wesley shows particular concern for these supposed reprobates, in that the doctrine of predestination leads some to believe or fear themselves to be among them, and therefore robbed from any joy or comfort in God. Because the die has already been cast, there is nothing one can do either to become one of the elect or to know that one is elect, and therefore Wesley sees it to be a cause of nihilism and despair—the opposite of the good news of life in Christ.

Related to his point on the destruction of holiness, Wesley says believing in predestination will also "destroy our zeal for good works."[11] His thinking is that if one is destined to eternal condemnation, what good will it do to tend to their current bodily needs? There is no hope of conversion, and no hope of saving their soul, and even if one is to better their lot in this life or extend it for some days or weeks or years, their ultimate fate is still damnation—so what's the point? A depressing conclusion indeed! The static, unchangeable certainty of predestination leaves no space for the agency of humanity, and therefore leads to nothing but futility in the spiritual life, whether regarding personal piety or works of mercy towards others. In Wesley's estimation, nothing seems worth doing at all if everything has already been decided since eternity and no change is possible.

Wesley argues that while proclaimers of predestination can in some way support their belief with Scripture, their doctrine ultimately goes against the "whole scope and tenor of Scripture."[12] For example, he says that using 2 Samuel 1:20's declaration that "Jacob I have loved, but Esau I have hated" as a literal dichotomy of salvation versus reprobation contradicts the larger picture and belief of God's loving all people and creation. Here Wesley gets most intense in his dispute. Given his consideration of and deep love and respect for Scripture, his belief that predestination contradicts it means he makes out Calvinists to be no less than blasphemers against God. Based in the ministry and death of Jesus Christ, Wesley's argument goes like this:

> Everywhere [Jesus] speaks *as if he was* willing that all men should be saved. Therefore, to say *he was not* willing that all men should be saved is to represent him as a mere hypocrite and dissembler. It can't be denied that the gracious words which came out of his mouth are full of invitations to all sinners. To say, then, he did not

11. Wesley, *Works* 3:550.
12. Wesley, *Works* 3:552.

intend to save all sinners is to represent him as a gross deceiver of the people.[13]

If all people were decidedly saved or damned from eternity, Wesley argues, then the work and words of Christ are nullified and, what's more, rendered untrue.

Ultimately, Wesley contends, the doctrine of predestination "destroys all [God's] attributes at once. It overturns both his justice, mercy, and truth." And it also "represents the most Holy God as worse than the devil; as both more false, more cruel, and more unjust."[14] In the same way that preaching is rendered moot in light of predestination, Wesley says the work of the devil is therefore useless—there are none for him to convince or connive, as it has already been established from eternity who will join him in hell, and God is the one who delivers them to the devil's hand. Therefore, predestination would be a boon to the devil, and therefore very evil indeed.

Even if one uses the Bible to defend the doctrine, Wesley denies that predestination can be proved by Scripture. Since predestination would make God out to be "worse than the devil," Wesley says, "it cannot be. Whatever that Scripture proves, it never can prove this. Whatever its true meaning be, this cannot be its true meaning."[15] In some sense, then, Wesley concedes that the Bible may seem to make a case for predestination. However, because the fact of predestination is so repugnant, and in the end makes God out to be evil rather than the perfect love that is God's true nature, that doctrine cannot be the true meaning of those verses or passages used to prove it. Wesley prioritizes God's love over anything the Scriptures might say to its contrary. "No Scripture can mean that God is not love," he says, "or that his mercy is not over all his works."[16] And therefore, since a scriptural proof of predestination would do just that, predestination cannot be proven by Scripture.

Wesley's assessment of the Calvinists is this:

> You still believe that in consequence of an unchangeable, irresistible decree of God the greater part of mankind abideth in death, without any possibility of redemption: inasmuch as none *can* save them but God; and he *will not* save them.[17]

13. Wesley, *Works* 3:554–55.
14. Wesley, *Works* 3:555.
15. Wesley, *Works* 3:556.
16. Wesley, *Works* 3:556.
17. Wesley, *Works* 3:547.

In predestining the elect to salvation, God has simultaneously elected the reprobate to damnation, such that God is pleased in the saving of some and glorified in the destruction of others. Wesley finds this portrait of God untenable. He refuses any doctrine asserting that a God whose nature and name is love could or would wantonly condemn God's beloved creatures.

To read "Free Grace" with a queer lens offers us a vision of the expansive love of a God who is encountered in the real, unpredictable, queer messiness of relationship. Wesley resists a God who plans creatures' destruction, who offers salvation to those to whom God refuses to give it. Wesley is committed to the queerness of freedom in relationship, of non-coercion, of denying the omnipotence of predestination, opting instead for the uncertainty of gracious love and true relationship. That God is love, for Wesley, means that God is open to the fullness of each human person, that God accepts and holds all of who we are, allowing us our autonomy and freedom without threatening, manipulating, or strong-arming us. Real love requires freedom.

A persistent marker of queerness is that it does not abide predetermined structures as normative for relationships. Queerness responds instead to the *reality* of things, how people *actually* show up in real life. As queer theologian Linn Tonstad describes it, "heterosexuality as a system doesn't deal with truth. Theological heterosexuality deals with fictions, ideas of what human beings ought to be like that are divorced and distanced from the reality of human, bodied, sexual life."[18] On the other hand, she says, "queer hermeneutics, queer ways of interpreting and knowing, search for the alternatives that are already there and that need to be found."[19] In contrast to heteronormative ways of thinking that assert simple, fixed rules for the way things are and the way things should be, queer thinking challenges us to identify and celebrate the oddities of the ways things truly are and the strange possibilities for how things could be.

Much of the appeal and comfort of predestination lie in its claims to certainty. The pre-decided course of all time and the universe has already been set and remains in the hands of a singularly powerful, sovereign God. Wesley bristles at this vision of God, questioning how it could accurately witness to a God who loves and has redeemed *all* of creation. Likewise, queerness questions the validity and the goodness of such a strictly ordered, calcified, and settled world and God. Certainly nothing is so certain.

---

18. Tonstad, *Queer Theology*, 76.

19. Tonstad, *Queer Theology*, 87.

We might read this dispute along the same lines of the common pro-LGBTQ+ argument that says a loving God would not create LGBTQ+ people just to then condemn them for being who they are. If God gave a person their LGBTQ+ identity, and all God's creation is indeed good, surely that same God would not consider the identity of God's creation to be a sin for which one is damned. Just as Wesley refuses to believe that God would lovingly create human beings who are destined for the hell of eternal condemnation, we might refuse to believe that God would lovingly create human beings who are destined for the hell of living a life contrary to their nature, or destined for eternal condemnation precisely because of the way God made them. This is a valid argument, and one that is used often in apologetics for LGBTQ+ inclusion in churches.

At the same time, we may also want to interrogate the implied staticity of sexuality and gender as identity markers and explore their dynamic fluidity. While many people argue that sexual identity is inherent, unchangeable, and not a choice (the "born this way" argument), there are other, more complex and nuanced ways of thinking about it as well. One challenge to the "born this way" narrative is the existence and experience of bi- or pansexuals and nonbinary or genderfluid individuals.[20]

In her book *Indecent Theology*, queer liberation theologian Marcella Althaus-Reid presents a model of what she calls the "Bi/Christ," a portrait of a Christ who challenges the binaries and either/or thinking that are reproduced by cis-heteropatriarchy. She asserts that the Christ of systematic theology is "a Christ of clear limits and boundaries, a compromise found amongst the ambiguities of his character and the almost military precision and clear planning of his life which heterosexual thought requires." On the other hand, the Bi/Christ is "a Christ who is neither this nor that, a Christ who embraces and shows life as fluid, changing, outside the reductionist patterns which confront people with irrelevant options."[21]

20. There is some discussion and disagreement in the LGBTQ+ community about the definitions of bi- and pansexuality. Some erroneously assume that the "bi" in bisexuality is transphobic or signifying a limitation to two genders—male and female. However, historically bisexuals have contended that the two "binary" poles of bisexuality are actually that of *my* gender and *other* genders. Some non-monosexuals use the label pansexual to sidestep this confusion. Additionally, pansexual is often used to indicate a person's attraction to all people *despite* their gender identity, whereas bisexuality is sometimes understood to include gender identity as an important part of sexual attraction. The distinction and use of these two terms is highly contextual and individual, so it is always advisable to ask others how they define them and which they prefer to use.

21. Althaus-Reid, *Indecent Theology*, 114.

Giving attention to bisexuality helps us expand our thinking, in that focusing on lesbian, gay, or even some binary transgender experience runs the risk of remaining caught in the trap of the same heteropatriarchal binary epistemology. In his introduction to his coedited volume on bisexualities, queer theorist Donald Hall says, "there are oh so many sexualities that do not fit into the reductive, though eminently useful, binary of hetero- and homosexuality."[22] In this way, bi- or pansexuality (and we might also include nonbinary and genderfluid gender expressions) is the queer of the queer. It resists not only the normative, binary rules of the hegemonic cis-heteropatriarchy, but also the normative, binary rules of all monosexuality. It insists on the multivalent multiplicity of gender and sexuality as it truly is and can be, rather than visions of what it "should" be.

In that same volume, Michael du Plessis says that "bisexuality runs counter to received notions about sexual identity as something in which the subject has no choice."[23] Counter to popular binary monosexual narratives, bi- and pansexuals have overwhelming choice in their selection of sexual, romantic, and domestic partners, and this process of unfolding exploration and unexpected surprise is part and parcel of their queer experience. Likewise, the way a nonbinary person *chooses* to dress and adorn themselves in presenting their identity to the world is never fixed or pre-decided but always in gorgeous flux, changing from day to day or even moment to moment. To assert that bi- or pansexuals and gender nonbinary people are born a certain way and therefore predestined to live or behave or appear a certain way is to demand their submission to oppression.

Many queer theorists understand queerness as an identity without an essence—that is, a shared claim to a shared way of being without some kernel of shared *something* that exists inherently in all such people. This allows not only for a broad understanding of queerness as a category, but also for a good deal of movement within, about, and around the category. Given that queerness cannot be reduced or collapsed into one essence, but instead explodes and multiplies and oozes uncontrollably, how are we to assert that queerness is ever a given, set, static, unchanging characteristic? Queerness refuses to be sentenced to a settled existence. It is unceasingly intent on becoming whatever it will be. A queerness that was imparted complete and fixed upon a person at (or before!) their birth is perhaps then no queerness at all.

22. Hall, "BI-Ntroduction II," 10.
23. Plessis, "Blatantly Bisexual," 41.

The theory of gender and sexual performativity popularized by theorist Judith Butler becomes significant here. The idea is that gender is not an inherent essence that is then expressed outwardly, but rather it is constructed by repeated symbolic action. Simone de Beauvoir's oft-cited quotation, "one is not born, but rather, becomes a woman," is an example of saying, as Butler does, that "gender is in no way a stable identity or locus of agency from which various acts proceed; rather, it is an identity tenuously constituted in time—an identity instituted through a *stylized repetition of acts*."[24] In other words, gender is not predetermined but rather is decided, from moment to moment, by socially conditioned acts and our socially constructed understanding of those acts as portraying gender. Gender is therefore constructed as it is performed. It is not a preexisting internal essence being expressed, nor a fixed external ideal we attempt to achieve, but rather our acts of gender create gender itself.[25] This self-constituting cycle brings into question our own subjectivity in this process, to be sure. While "social agents constitute social reality through language, gesture, and all manner of symbolic social sign," we are not always or only the subject of the acts, but we are also their object.[26] So as we construct our genders by our actions, they construct us—bodies and minds—into our genders, such that we become convinced of their necessity. We become convinced that one is "born male," that the binary is "natural," that sex, gender, and sexuality are predestined.

That Wesley denies predestination means he believes in people's power and agency to respond to God's grace of their own volition. God does not strong-arm people into holiness, nor does God leave people purposely, hopelessly unredeemed. The same might be said regarding gender and sexuality. We are not inherently, unchangeably destined to *be* any gender or sexuality. In a queer understanding, our gender and sexual identities are not inexorably founded in fixed and essential fact or biology, but rather are fluid and dynamic communal performances in which we get to participate.

Just as Wesley's Arminian doctrine spurs us toward responsibility, holiness, and joy rather than the indifference, hopelessness, and despair he sees in Calvinist predestination, queerness leaves open to us endless

---

24. Butler, "Performative Acts and Gender Constitution," 519. Butler's theory of gender performativity is more thoroughly delineated in her 1990 book *Gender Trouble*, though this article is an early and succinct rehearsal of it.

25. Butler, "Performative Acts and Gender Constitution," 522.

26. Butler, "Performative Acts and Gender Constitution," 519.

possibilities for the ways we respond to our social world and its calls on us to account for our gender and sexuality. We are not doomed for all time to a preset, "natural" gender or sexuality that is interior, intrinsic, and integral to us, one that somehow not only corresponds exactly to every person who shares our gender but also is in perfect opposition to those whose gender is our "opposite." In Wesley's sermon, he emphasizes God's love above all when it comes to redemption, which he believes must be authentic and responsive to the messiness of real life rather than playing out of an unworkable predetermined ideal. If we are to love our neighbors, seek holiness, and find joy in our relation to God, it means releasing the comfort found in the certainty of predestination in favor of responding to the invitation to participation in struggling to work out our salvation by the grace of God. As feminist theologians Lisa Isherwood and Dorothea McEwan muse, "religion is not about standing still, repeating established 'truths,' being limited by accepted interpretations; religion is about the communion of community in the present, the interrelatedness of everybody, connecting and networking, carrying and caring."[27] The relationship of being a Christian in Christian community, as Wesley sees it, is not established on predestined, unchanging, frozen "truths," but is expressed in the ever-changing struggle of learning to love people as they are, and responding to the expanding, expansive grace of God.

As Wesleyans, this theology will extend to our understanding of human sexuality as well. If all things have not been established from eternity, if we are active agents who share responsibility with God in creating our world and ourselves, then the way we perform our gender and sexuality with and for and around others is an open-ended question that we get to answer in myriad ways. Rather than unilaterally establishing our personality, preferences, and proclivities from eternity, God in God's love graciously opens up all worlds to us, inviting us to respond by exploring and inhabiting our bodies in whatever ways multiply that grace and love that has gone before us. Whenever we choose to respond to God's prevenient grace and love with our own grace and love, we are participating in God's holiness. And, naturally, such response can and must take infinite and indefinite forms. It can be seen in the love between people, whose genders may be the same or different or somehow both, combinations and permutations as diverse as the people involved. Even this love might be expressed in innumerable ways, from a look to a meal to a touch to an ecstatic exchange of

27. Isherwood and McEwan, *Introducing Feminist Theology*, 75.

the interpermeabilities of flesh. It can be seen in the slow process of inter-rogating oneself, one's desires, one's being, and responding by growing into a more truthful form of embodiment or expression. That any of the variants of gender and sexuality and their exploration and expression could be un-movably set in stone at any point in a person's life, much less down through eternity, is indeed, as Wesley says, a blasphemy. To hold such a belief is to hold a belief in a God who is stuck, who is limited. This God cannot be the God of love, for true love requires the flex and bend and warmth and breath of the messiness of real life and its ever-undulating contours.

In queering Wesley's stance and struggle against Calvinist predestina-tion, we can also struggle against the belief that individuals' genders and sexualities, as well as their rightness or wrongness, are likewise predestined. We can question the "naturalness" or inherent insistence of a gender bi-nary, or of compulsory heterosexuality. We can proclaim that nothing is fixed, and certainly not fixed toward condemnation. A queer Wesley insists that the God of love is a God who, in prevenient grace, flings open every possibility and invites us to participate, leaving space for exploration and experimentation in a field where there are no right answers besides the sim-plicity of holy love, and that within that love there is unlimited potential. The love of God is an invitation to wholeness. God does not create in order to condemn, but in order to make love and real relationship possible. We are freed by free grace to respond in and toward our own freedom.

A CAUTION AGAINST BIGOTRY

In his introduction to this sermon, Albert Outler presents its context: After the English Civil War of the seventeenth century, there had been a general atmosphere of peace and a suspicion of any excess of partisan or religious zeal or bigotry, which Wesley defined as "too strong an attachment to, or fondness for, our own party, opinion, church, and religion."[1] So with the appearance and growth of the Methodist movement and their enthusiastic revivals came accusations of their "bigotry." While Outler asserts that Wesley "studiously avoids an apologetic stance," it is nevertheless clear in Wesley's argument for plurality and tolerance that he is intent on making space for his own work and for other differences of opinion and practice in the church. Given this, we can read the sermon as a case for affirming spaces for LGBTQ+ people and for the value of the ministry of LGBTQ+ clergy and laypeople.

This sermon takes as its text Mark 9:38–39, part of a short interlude wherein the apostle John tells Jesus, "Teacher, we saw someone driving out demons in your name and we told him to stop, because he was not one of us." Ostensibly, John is seeking favor and praise. He assumes he has done something right in defining who is among the followers of Jesus and who is therefore properly credentialed for demon-driving. However, Jesus' answer comes off as surprising. "Do not stop him," Jesus says, "For no one who does a miracle in my name can in the next moment say anything bad about me." He goes on to say in verses 40 and 41, "Whoever is not against us is for us. Truly I tell you, anyone who gives you a cup of water in my name because you belong to the Messiah will certainly not lose their reward." Instead of receiving a pat on the back for his judicious gatekeeping, John is rebuffed. What he had thought was loyalty is dismissed. The person was

---

1. Wesley, *Works* 2:62.

successfully driving out demons, and they were doing so in the name of Jesus. That seems to be enough for Jesus to consider them legitimate, or at least not illegitimate.

This interchange is placed only a few verses after Jesus himself drives out a demon. A desperate father says his son has been possessed by a demon, and he had asked the disciples to drive it out, but they could not (Mark 9:18). The disciples' apparent lack of facility with demons becomes more glaring when it is revealed that another healer, one who is decidedly "not one of us," has this power by Jesus' name that it seems the disciples themselves—those who are Jesus' inner circle, his truest followers—cannot always access. Perhaps it is jealousy, or possessiveness of Jesus' powers, that caused John to desire a stop to this other man's healing work.

Directly after these verses, Jesus talks about causing others to stumble, saying that "If anyone causes one of these little ones—those who believe in me—to stumble, it would be better for them if a large millstone were hung around their neck and they were thrown into the sea" (Mark 9:42). Whether these words have as their referent the little child Jesus welcomes in verse 36, or anyone who would do miracles or offer a cup of water in his name, the meaning is clear. Jesus is dissuading his disciples from barring or otherwise disrupting the progress or work of any who would identify with him and do his work of casting out demons. His forceful, perhaps hyperbolic, words indicate a desire for openness, community, diversity—the little ones, the outsiders, all kinds should be allowed to come into his orbit, to use his name for the care and healing of the world. He would not have his name, his power, his care denied to them.

The frame provided by the demon-possessed boy and the threat of drowning for keeping someone from righteousness serves to fill out the otherwise scarce anecdote of the demon-fighting outsider. Both of the framing narratives have elements of the interior narrative which Wesley takes as his text. On the front end, the presence of the demon, and the exercise of casting it out, ties Jesus' action of successful healing with that of the outsider. And on the other end, the caution against prohibition of one who *would* be "one of us," who would do miracles if they were not forbidden, ties the disciples' forbidding of the outsider with the causing to stumble of one of the "little ones" who would believe in Jesus. The framing narratives reinforce both the legitimacy of the outsider's work and the injunction against forbidding them.

Wesley's sermon of this gospel text takes shape in three parts:

1. In what sense people cast out devils

2. How to understand "he followeth not us"

3. Explanation of the Lord's direction "forbid him not"

Like many people today, Wesley identifies a difference in the existence and behavior of "devils" in the biblical stories and his experience of "devils" in his own world. He makes the distinction that in the time of the Bible, the devil "tormented their bodies as well as souls, and that openly, without any disguise," but that now he "torments their souls only (unless in some rare cases) and that as covertly as possible."[2] The so-called "Prince of this world" rules over people "by keeping possession of their hearts, setting up his throne there, and bringing every thought into obedience to himself."[3] Those who are possessed by the devil rather than God are considered wicked, in that they are marked by the corruption of the image of God in them. The image of God is first holiness, which is primarily love. So the chief mark of wickedness, of the possession by devils, must be unlove.

What could we say about devils today? Do they possess or affect the body or the mind? Perhaps now that we understand more clearly the inexorability of mind and body—that the mind is part of the body, that the body affects the mind—we might understand "devils" to affect us in a similarly integrated way.

The devil, Wesley says, "chains their souls down to earth and hell with the chains of their own vile affections."[4] These devils, then, may be possessive, obsessive thoughts and behaviors marked by evil rather than love, condemnation rather than grace. The devils may be anything that obscures or denies freedom and wholeness. They keep people from "reaching heaven" due to their own misguided feelings—of inadequacy, despair, hate for others. To cast out devils is to free the captive, to liberate those held down and held back by oppression and harm and unlove.

By way of example or case study regarding devils and their casting out, I'd like to consider the mental health struggles of LGBTQ+ people as a model of the "demons" that run rampant in the world and possess the souls and bodies of people today.

Much qualitative and quantitative research has been done exploring the mental health experiences and outcomes of LGBTQ+ people, including

2. Wesley, *Works* 2:65.

3. Wesley, *Works* 2:64.

4. Wesley, *Works* 2:66.

youth, and their involvement in religious communities. A recent study says that sexual minority youth "reported significantly higher rates of suicidality and depression symptoms as compared with the heterosexual youth."[5] Fergusson et al. concluded that "gay, lesbian, and bisexual young people are at increased risk of mental health problems, with these associations being particularly evident for measures of suicidal behavior and multiple disorder."[6] Combining this already at-risk population with religious involvement produces striking results. On the one hand, queer folks who attended non-affirming churches have been shown to have even higher rates of mental health issues. Hatzenbuehler et al. "found that LGB youth living in counties [in Oregon] that had higher concentrations of nonaffirming faith communities had increased rates of alcohol abuse."[7] Hamblin and Gross found that "attending a nonaffirming church is associated with symptoms of anxiety in lesbian and gay adults."[8] They also said that "participation in conservative or rejecting religious communities may adversely affect the emotional well-being of GL [gay and lesbian] individuals."[9] On the other hand, studies have also shown the positive outcomes of LGBTQ+ people in affirming church spaces. Rodriguez and Ouellette report that "involvement at [Metropolitan Community Church in New York City], for both gay men and lesbians, is

---

5. Marshal et al., "Suicidality and Depression Disparities Between Sexual Minority and Heterosexual Youth."

6. Fergusson et al., "Is Sexual Orientation Related to Mental Health Problems and Suicidality in Young People?," 876.

7. Wolff et al., "Sexual Minority Students in Non-Affirming Religious Higher Education," 202.

8. Wolff et al., "Sexual Minority Students in Non-Affirming Religious Higher Education," 202.

9. "[T]heir religious organization's view of homosexuality, perceived conflict between religious faith identity and sexual orientation identity, social support, depression, and generalized anxiety. Among participants who rated their church as rejecting of homosexuality, greater frequency of attendance was related to a higher incidence of GAD symptoms, but not depression. No correlation was found for those attending accepting faith communities. Those who attend rejecting faith communities attended services less often, experienced greater identity conflict, and reported significantly less social support than those of the Accepted group. Regression analyses indicated that identity conflict and social support did not fully account for the relationship between attendance and GAD symptoms. Overall, findings from the current study support previous suggestions that participation in conservative or rejecting religious communities may adversely affect the emotional well-being of GL individuals." Hamblin and Gross, "Role of Religious Attendance and Identity Conflict in Psychological Well-Being," 825.

an important means of identity integration for many of the participants."[10] Further, they point out that "all but five of those participants who reported identity integration claimed that MCC/NY helped them to realize and maintain a sense of themselves as both gay/lesbian and Christian."[11] That is, the participants' involvement with the church had a direct effect on their positive, holistic understanding and acceptance of themselves.

Though these studies vary widely in many aspects—their ages, their sample size and populations, their goals, and their methodologies—when they are considered together, we can construct a fairly cohesive picture: LGBTQ+ people, particularly youth, experience higher levels of mental health issues than their cisgender, straight counterparts; participation in non-affirming religious communities exacerbates these issues, while participation in affirming spaces contributes to their healing.

If we think about mental health issues as an example of the demons present in our world today, it is worth considering the ability (or lack thereof) of Jesus' disciples to cast them out. If nonaffirming churches are contributing to the "demon possession" of LGBTQ+ people by mental health issues, then it stands to reason they will not be able to drive them out. To cross-reference and paraphrase Matthew 12:26, how can Satan cast out Satan? Perhaps indeed it will take others, those who "followeth not us," to do the work of undoing the demonic harm that Jesus' disciples have wrought on their LGBTQ+ kin. Perhaps it is precisely the work of those whom Jesus' disciples have identified as other, as aberrant, as contrary, that may drive out these demons that Jesus' disciples themselves have invoked. In this read, then, those "others" may be affirming churches and denominations as well as queer clergy and laypeople. The ones who are nonaffirming or "traditional" disciples have cast aspersions on these others, convinced that they could not possibly be authorized to heal in Jesus' name since they are not of the "correct" beliefs or practices. They try to stop these others from ministering, from caring for and healing the demons of LGBTQ+ people. But the word of Jesus is decisive: "Do not stop them." The healing done by these others, the casting out of these powerful and corrosive and life-threatening demons, is not only legitimate, but indeed desperately needed. And these others are able to reach those demons that the "traditional" disciples cannot touch.

10. Rodriguez and Ouellette, "Gay and Lesbian Christians," 344.

11. Rodriguez and Ouellette, "Gay and Lesbian Christians," 342.

Affirming spaces have been proven to lessen these demons in LG-BTQ+ youth. Meanwhile, nonaffirming spaces harbor and propagate them, infecting God's children and driving them toward destruction. Who then is it who really "followeth not us"? Who is not working in accordance with Jesus and the one he calls his Father? To cast out these devils is to inject their victims with love and compassion, to welcome them with the light of the Holy Spirit, the care of community, and the liberation made flesh in Jesus and his kingdom. To be free from these devils is to be truly free and truly oneself—part of the humanity that fully images God. "It is God alone who can cast out Satan," Wesley says.[12] Therefore if Satan is being cast out, if people are being healed from their possession by the devils that torment them, if evil is abating, it must be the work of God.

The presence and experience of LGBTQ+ clergy go a long way in driving these devils from the lives of their parishioners, particularly those who are also LGBTQ+. In the same way, the visibility of and identification with female clergy affects the faith and spiritual lives of women and girls. Seeing other LGBTQ+ people live out God's calling on their lives in ministry can impart hope and dignity to LGBTQ+ people in the pews. What's more, perhaps queer clergy are especially empowered to cast out devils that cisgender, heterosexual ministers can't touch. Just as the disciples could not cast the devil out of the boy in Mark 9, perhaps there are limits to the reach of straight clergy's ministry, and queer clergy and lay ministers are necessary for filling in these gaps.

In the second part of this sermon, Wesley questions what it means for the other healers in the passage not to be following Jesus and his disciples. He points out the several different ways one might understand this not-following: that they don't have personal acquaintance with him, that he is of a different party, that he holds different opinions, that he observes different practices, that he is not a Christian at all, or that he is in opposition to them. He recognizes that these states of difference can indeed be significant. Regarding the material consequence of conflict, he says, "The differences which begin in points of opinion seldom terminate there."[13] Wesley is under no illusion about the diversity of opinion and practice within the church. He is quite comfortable to acknowledge the wide breadth of perspectives and beliefs even within otherwisely sympatico assemblies. In fact, he muses, given the infinite variety of opinions people may hold in the church, it is

12. Wesley, *Works* 2:68.
13. Wesley, *Works* 2:72.

entirely possible that "whenever we see *anyone* 'casting out devils' he will be one that in this sense 'followeth not us'—that is not of our opinion."[14] There is no way to ensure that any given person doing the work of the Lord in the world will be of precisely the same mind as every other person, except that they have the mind of Christ—whose body is constituted in its infinite variety of the people of God. Wesley makes this point that difference (perhaps indeed queerness) is inherent in the church, and that we must recognize it and allow it breathing room. Even this core commonality does not mean there will not be those who, in some way, "followeth not us." It is not only impossible to have a church entirely unified in its beliefs, but also perhaps it is not even desirable. There are certainly differences that may be so deep as to create true opposition and enmity, but Wesley does not believe this to be the case in this instance since they are still doing miracles in Christ's name. And the fact of the diversity of ideas and opinions even within a relatively unified church means that difference in itself cannot be enough to necessitate a prohibition or an excommunication.

Wesley does point out several types of people who most clearly followeth not us: "children of disobedience," people who do the work of the devil: "common swearers, drunkards, whoremongers, adulterers, thieves, robbers, sodomites, murderers."[15] This is the only one of all of his sermons to include any reference to "sodomy." In this sense, we might say it is the closest we get to an explicit treatment by Wesley of "homosexuality." However, it is important to consider what Wesley might mean by his use of "sodomite," and the implications of such a word and its attendant historical conceptualizations of sexuality.

The list of evildoers would seem to be a fairly typical list of moral failures. However, it occurs directly after Wesley mentions other examples of evildoers: the Creeks, Cherokees, and Chickasaws. Wesley paints a gross caricature of Native Americans, saying that they take prisoners to torture and roast, that they have no loyalty to their own people, that they become tired of their children and so drown them.[16] It is worth interrogating Wesley's sense of reality when it comes to these supposedly common works of the devil in his world. The prejudiced and mostly unfounded colonialist assumptions Wesley places on Native Americans should also give us pause when considering the other enumerated "works of the devil." What does

14. Wesley, *Works* 2:70.

15. Wesley, *Works* 2:67–68.

16. Wesley, *Works* 2:67.

he think is going on here? And is there any evidence it is really happening? These questions become even more relevant when addressed toward activities taking place behind closed doors.

The historical ideological slipperiness of sodomy as a category of sin must be considered if we are going to assert its meaningfulness in any conversation about sexuality. Mark Jordan's excellent book *The Invention of Sodomy* makes obvious the inherent instability of the term and its use. He asserts that the category of sodomy "is confused and contradictory in just the way that oppressors and demagogues find advantageous," implying that the word and the concept is used in whatever way is expedient for the powerful's quashing of any unwanted behavior or whisper of sexual pleasure. Because throughout history "sodomy" has been used to mean all kinds of things and also nothing at all, Jordan concludes that "the category 'sodomy' cannot be used for serious thinking."[17] Indeed, he says, ultimately "'sodomy' is a name not for a kind of human behavior, but for a failure of theologians."[18] When it comes to sodomy, it appears that there's no "there" there, and so to use it as the basis for a theological argument about sin or morality appears to be irresponsible or even foolish.

For this reason, we can be grateful that Wesley does not appeal to arguments against "sodomy" but this once. Perhaps he also sensed the shadowy, imprecise nature of the term, and therefore spent his time addressing the other, more pressing and more obvious concerns of his audiences. It would certainly be more consistent with his work and witness to give the bulk of his attention to the prophet Ezekiel's definition of sodomy: "This was the sin of your sister Sodom: She and her daughters were arrogant, overfed and unconcerned; they did not help the poor and needy" (Ezek 16:49). Wesley could indeed be referring to such evildoing in this very use of the word "sodomite." It's not clear. And while I don't want to make an argument from silence, it is therefore challenging to give an adequate treatment of Wesley's understanding and rejection of "sodomy" given the sparseness of its mention and the concept's own historical instability. We can perhaps assume Wesley's general opposition to any kind of same-sex sexual activity, and probably much sexual activity in general, given the social conventions of his time. But precisely because this assumed attitude is based in his social milieu rather than his work itself, it warrants interrogation.[19]

17. Jordan, *Invention of Sodomy*, 9.

18. Jordan, *Invention of Sodomy*, 176.

19. Peter Forsaith's article, ". . . too indelicate to mention . . .," addresses just this

LGBTQ+ Christians and our affirming allies have often been accused of not following Jesus, or of not following him in a manner that is acceptable to some of his disciples. We have been marginalized, ostracized, barred from ministry, and barred from worship. We have been overscrutinized and underappreciated, regarded with suspicion and distrust. We know what it's like to be told to stop because we were different, because we were not an accepted part of an approved "us" created precisely on the principle of excluding those who are different. Given the various ways Wesley outlines that one might fall outside the parameters of "following," difference in opinion and practice regarding LGBTQ+ people can serve as a prime example of the kind of difference that some disciples may call into question. They could very well assume that LGBTQ+ people or their allies fall into any or all of the not-following categories that Wesley enumerates. But it's less important to consider why the disciples thought these others were not on their team and more important to focus on Jesus' response to them in favor of these others: "Forbid them not."

In this third part of the sermon, these queer others whom the disciples were so quick and proud to quash are defended by Jesus and by Wesley. Wesley's affirmation of Jesus' encouragement is decisive:

> Do not in any wise strive to prevent his using all the power which God has given him. If you have authority with him, do not use that authority to stop the work of God. Do not furnish him with reasons why he ought not any more to speak in the name of Jesus.[20]

If one is doing the work of God, it matters not whether they are part of this group or that, in your party or another. The work of God, that is the casting out of devils, is to be encouraged and affirmed in all of its ways and at the hands of all who would do it. The propensity to limit and control who is allowed to do what in the church is an age-old tendency. But, Wesley muses, "Shall not God work by whom he will work?" and further, "if God hath sent him, will you call him back?"[21] These words are a challenge to those disciples who would forbid the ministry of queer others, who would question God's presence or call on their lives when the fruit of their work is obvious and abundant. Ultimately, we Wesleyans believe it is God who grants God's gifts to God's people, and therefore we must submit to the

---

question, investigating Wesley's and other Methodists' knowledge of, aid to, and compassion toward criminally accused sodomites in eighteenth-century Oxford.

20. Wesley, *Works* 2:73.

21. Wesley, *Works* 2:73.

wisdom of the Holy Spirit, and recognize those gifts that have been be-
stowed to all kinds of people, near and far, within and without our imagined boxes of categorization.

In fact, it appears that the ones who are not of God are actually those
who would forbid those workers of God outside their own group. Their prohibitions are more akin to the work of the devil, who Wesley says, "blinds
the eyes of their understanding so that the light of the glorious gospel of
Christ cannot shine upon them."[22] In forbidding others to do the work of
God, these disciples are preventing the gospel from being preached, and
preventing the healing love of God from reaching those who need it most.
This kind of reversal is not uncommon in what we understand as the Kingdom of God. Jesus is often on the side of the marginalized. So it should
not be surprising that he comes to the defense of these outsiders who were
doing the very kind of healing that he himself had been sent to do.

Wesley speaks then at length about discerning whether others have
a calling from God, whether that call must be "outward" or if "inward"
only may suffice. Ultimately, he concludes that if a person is found to be
holy, if they have gifts that may edify the church, and if they are bringing sinners to repentance, then he is convinced they should be allowed to
conduct their ministry. He recognizes that many such people are, for one
reason or another, refused ordination, but that given his interpretation of
this passage, he would not be the one to refuse them. He asserts that if the
bishop will not ordain the person, then "the bishop does 'forbid him to
cast out devils.' But I dare not forbid him."[23] The implication for LGBTQ+
Christians here should be obvious. Those of us who are called by God to be
ministers, to serve God's people and cast out devils, who strive to live holy
lives and preach the gospel and offer our gifts in service to the church, are
routinely forbidden. We are denied ordination to which we are otherwise
qualified and called. We are disallowed from roles of leadership and service
as laypeople. We are blackballed, blackmailed, and blacklisted, despite our
demonstrable abilities and the church's need for our gifts.

Wesley includes a lengthy list of the ways disciples might forbid the
queer others whom Jesus permits:

> You indirectly forbid him if you either wholly deny, or despise and
> make little account of the work which God has wrought by his
> hands. You indirectly forbid him when you discourage him in his

22. Wesley, *Works* 2:66.
23. Wesley, *Works* 2:75.

work by drawing him into disputes concerning it, by raising objections against it, or frighting him with consequences which very possibly will never be. You forbid him when you show any unkindness toward him either in language or behaviour; and much more when you speak of him to others either in an unkind or a contemptuous manner, when you endeavour to represent him to any either in an odious or a despicable light. You are forbidding him all the time you are speaking evil of him or making no account of his labours.[24]

No doubt these methods of forbidding sound very familiar to Wesleyan LGBTQ+ laypeople and clergy. Who among us has not had their work denied, despised, or belittled? Who among us has not been drawn into disputes, demanded to give an account of ourselves and our faith and our humanity? Who among us has not had objections raised to us, or been threatened with empty consequences for living in alignment with our calling and conscience? Who among us has not been shown unkindness, or had such unkindness spoken of us behind our backs? Queer Christians have had our work and witness forbidden by so-called disciples over and over again. And the message of Wesley and Jesus is clear: Don't.

The dynamic of this passage, of the rejecting of those who are attempting to do good, reminds me of the prohibition of gay men and sex workers from donating blood. The Red Cross bars from donation any "male who has had sexual contact with another male, in the last twelve months," or anyone who has *ever* received payment for sex.[25] This discrimination fails to take into consideration myriad aspects of such people's lives, behaviors, and actual practice, instead relying on ignorant judgment and assumptions, and in doing so limits the reach of the possible healing that could result from these individuals' offerings. The rule unnecessarily turns away every year an unknown number of healthy, willing donors, whose blood could save lives. Meanwhile, the organization bemoans a lack of donors, often publicizing that it is experiencing a critical shortage of blood to give. In the same way, Wesleyan churches complain about decreasing Sunday worship attendance, and a lack of talented and educated ministers. Meanwhile, the LGBTQ+ faithful are rejected, demeaned, and pushed out, despite their hunger for holiness, their ministerial skill, and their desire to serve.

24. Wesley, *Works* 2:75–76.

25. See the "Eligibility Criteria" page on the Red Cross website: https://www.redcross-blood.org/donate-blood/how-to-donate/eligibility-requirements/eligibility-criteria-alphabetical.html.

Wesleyan churches are sending away the very blood that could save their lives and revitalize their congregations.

Wesley entreats us to "encourage whomsoever God is pleased to employ."[26] We gain nothing by limiting the reach of God's love and grace. The disciples' pride at having stopped a healer from helping suffering people should seem foolish because it is. And it should give us pause to consider that Wesleyan churches are similarly denying the distressed healing by rejecting the gifts of LGBTQ+ clergy and laypeople. Queer folks have rich and abundant gifts to offer our church, if the other disciples of Jesus would simply stop forbidding us. Whatever differences exist between our beliefs and practices, if we are working for the healing and wholeness of others in Jesus' name, if our goal is holiness and love, we are in the same family and on the same team, and we should be encouraged and empowered rather than restricted. Wesley calls on us to remember the instruction of Jesus to "forbid them not" and make room in the church for the diverse beliefs and bodies and practices and perspectives that make up Christ's body, which is ultimately for the world and its healing.

26. Wesley, *Works* 2:77.

THE IMPERFECTION
OF HUMAN KNOWLEDGE

A common misunderstanding and critique of the Wesleyan tradition's concept of Christian perfection lies in the word *perfection*, and in the assumption that to attain this kind of perfection means, in part, to attain perfect knowledge—that is, *to know everything*. However, virtually no one lives under the illusion that such a feat is possible. The frustrating finitude of our humanity is well-known to us. In this sermon, John Wesley argues for human ignorance—that there is so much we don't know, and so much we don't even know that we don't know. Therefore, he reasons, this ignorance should spur us toward humility, confidence in God who is in all places and knows all things, and resignation and rest in God's will. But Wesley does not only focus on the limits of our knowledge. He also highlights the fact that we are nonetheless always seeking and yearning for more. "Although our desire of knowledge has no bounds," he says, "yet our knowledge itself has."[1] Our capacity for knowledge may be limited, but our desire for it is not.

Wesley's assertion of ignorance is not an embrace of obliviousness or an admonition against learning. On the contrary, Wesley's own inquisitive mind and desire for knowledge had him reading and learning constantly—about the natural and social worlds as well as the spiritual. He studied and wrote extensively about biology and medicine, astronomy, literature, and politics. One of Wesley's most popular publications was his *Primitive Physick*, subtitled, "an easy and natural method for curing most diseases." And while more spiritually focused than typical medical literature, it was fairly consistent with the mainstream medical literature of its time. Wesley was an enthusiastic proponent of education, and he found the pursuit of

1. Wesley, *Works* 2:568.

scientific knowledge—particularly as it supported people's lives and wellbe-ing—to be a worthwhile endeavor, the goal being ultimately to seek a better understanding of God's creation and God as creator. In Wesley's view, be-cause God is the author of all creation and all knowledge, it is as boundless indeed as Godself. And our desire to know is equally as boundless, though ultimately there are limits to what we can know as finite human beings.

There may be something queer about this unbounded desire, and something queer about the tragedy of its limited satiability. We may be filled, but not with the fullness. Our cup is too small to hold all we would drink. But the want has no limits. The knowledge has no limits. They stretch out in all directions, ever unfolding and expanding as the universe. What's more, our *ways* of knowing are likewise boundless. The uniqueness of per-spectives granted us by each person's individual way of thinking, seeing, experiencing the world means there is no limit to the ways we can know even the tiniest portion of reality. And given this glorious multiplicity of angles on the world, establishing artificial yet immovable borders to limit what knowledge we might gain is foolish, if not cruel. The imperfection of our knowledge should encourage us to revel in what we have, to follow our desires as far as they will go, to explore and learn as much as we can without fear or discrimination.

This sermon reads as a litany of questions. Wesley asks questions about light, air, the earth, the "vegetable kingdom," animals—including mi-croscopic animals, insects, and beasts—the human soul, the body, the flesh, and dreams. In all of these categories, he lists the mysteries that confound humanity as proof that our knowledge is limited.

Wesley would be pleased and amazed to find that two-and-a-half cen-turies later, humanity has continued to ask, and indeed has found answers to, many of the questions he poses in this sermon. For example, the study of light and its wave-particle duality has had numerous breakthroughs, es-pecially in the early twentieth century with the advent of quantum physics. "How much do we know of that wonderful body, *light*?" Wesley asks. "Does it flow in a continued stream from the sun? Or does the sun impel the particles next his orb, and so on and on, to the extremity of his system?"[2] Wesley's question of whether light was a wave or a particle is at the center of the quantum question, and the queerness of the answers continue to unfold in labs and imaginations today. From Newton to Hooke, through Maxwell

2. Wesley, *Works* 2:572.

and Einstein, physicists have proven light to be *both* wave and particle, though neither conclusion has displaced the other completely.

The best demonstration of light's duality is through the so-called double-slit experiment. The experiment was first developed and performed in 1801 by Thomas Young, as a way to prove that light was a wave. However, as the field of physics and its attendant technology evolved, the experiment proved also to show the photons of light to behave as individual particles. The difference lies in the mode of observation. In the experiment, light is projected through two slits onto a surface, where one can observe the interference pattern generated by the light acting as waves.[3] Previous to Young's experiment, Newton and others had posited that light was made of particles. That Wesley was aware of this conversation even at the writing of this sermon in 1784 shows that even then it was not considered a settled matter. When scientists decided to look more closely during the experiment and measure *which* slit the photons were traveling through as they were projected, the pattern generated on the surface was not one of a wave, but of two discrete lines. When someone had their eye on them, the photons acted differently—indeed *became different*. This experiment has been the queer bedrock of quantum mechanics ever since. It turns out that even the modernist bulwark of science contains within itself a foundational unknowing. The imperfection of human knowledge is part and parcel of the endeavor of defining the mysteries of the universe.

Wesley lived in the early modernist world of Newtonian physics, whose namesake, Sir Isaac Newton, was born just sixty years before Wesley himself, and in the same country. Classical Newtonian physics fundamentally assumes "that the world is composed of individual objects with individually determined boundaries and properties."[4] This orderly, stable assumption of the natural world ruled the scientific imagination of the time, and has continued to be incredibly influential in the study of science, but also in the popular Western way of thinking about the world. It has served to bring countless scientific, and particularly medical, breakthroughs that have increased lifespans and standards of living the world over. And while this system has been more or less useful on the macro-scientific level, as science progressed to increasingly complex and granular questions, physicists have found that once we get down to the subatomic nitty-gritty, Newtonian

---

3. For more on the double-slit experiment, see Karen Barad's *Meeting the Universe Halfway*, or any of the many excellent animated demonstrations on YouTube.

4. Barad, *Meeting the Universe Halfway*, 107.

physics won't cut it. Quantum physics calls everything into question. Wesley's concern about light's wave-particle duality is an example: it turns out that light exists as *both* wave and particle and cannot be once and for all classified as one or the other.

The analogy of Newtonian/Quantum to normative/queer follows readily. The Newtonian view of science and the world has dominated the Western imagination for centuries, creating hard and fast distinctions, categories, laws, and rules that shape how we understand reality. In fact, this Newtonian reality includes the way we have come to understand gender and sexuality in binary, definitive terms. And so as it becomes apparent that reality at the quantum level is much stranger and unknown and uncontainable than we previously assumed, it should follow that the reality of gender and sexuality is the same. The supposed limits of someone's expression and performance of gender, or of the possible or appropriate ways to experience love and pleasure with our bodies, are far weirder and variable and surprising and exciting than we ever could have guessed. The calcified norms of "male" and "female," of compulsory monogamy and heterosexuality, that were established and maintained by the Newtonian worldview, are therefore challenged by the introduction of new knowledge. And as we dig in and continue to pursue the questions and explore the possibilities that have hitherto seemed impossible, the more we see the sparkling, glorious boundlessness of knowledge, even knowledge of ourselves.

Feminist philosopher of science Karen Barad has an excellent article that explores the dynamic shiftiness of the natural world. In "Nature's Queer Performativity," Barad gives several examples of the unpredictable, unsettled weirdness of nature to argue that queer sex, so-called "acts against nature," are no such thing given that nature itself is quite queer. Her argument supports Wesley's and allows us to see the queerness in it. Barad introduces us to such "queer critters" as *Pfiesteria piscicida*, "a bizarre one-celled predator that can appear to transform itself from animal to plant and back again."[5] Similar to light, which may appear as wave or as particle depending on the variables of measurement, the *Pfiesteria*'s very being materializes differently depending on the circumstances. And even then not in a deterministic way that can be predicted. Barad therefore makes the distinction between epistemological uncertainty—that is, our own inability to know or understand a singular, solid truth—and ontological indeterminacy—that the very *being* of that truth is actually not settled or certain to be known

5. Barad, "Nature's Queer Performativity," 133.

in the first place. It is not only or simply our own limited knowledge that makes it difficult to pin down the nature of reality, but the ever-changing, shifting, growing nature of reality itself.

As scientists have studied the biology, neurology, chemistry, and psychology of sexuality and gender, they have found such study to reveal more questions than answers. Anne Fausto-Sterling's excellent little book *Sex/Gender: Biology in a Social World* gives an overview of just how complicated our bodies and brains are in this regard. In it, she reveals the grossly oversimplified question of nature versus nurture, or biology versus society, to be infinitely layered and complex, with so many variables and moving parts that any attempt to definitively answer it is a fool's errand. For example, summarizing the development of a fetus, she explains that "a newborn is a multilayered sexual creature, the result of having a chromosomal sex, a fetal gonadal sex, fetal hormonal sex, a fetal internal reproductive sex, a brain sex, an external genital sex, and, starting from the moment the child leaves the womb, a developing body image and social gender fortification."[6] All of these pieces combine with chance to produce a person's biological make-up at birth. But it doesn't stop there. Chemicals and tissues and hormones continue to change as we grow up and grow old, and so do the stories we tell about them, to ourselves and others. Just like the dinoflagellate *Pfiesteria*, our own sexual being is constructed by a multitude of influences, "not simply deterministic causality."[7] Add in the vagaries of attraction and love, and it's a wonder anyone would dream of asserting a supposedly solid, unchangeable fact about any of it. In this sense, Wesley's musing stands: "As to our *body* itself, how little do we know!"[8]

To Wesley's point, what we know and what we don't know are both constantly in flux; the entire enterprise of *knowing* itself comes into question when we consider the Enlightenment subject of modernity, the neoliberal subject of late capitalism, the postcolonial colonized subject, and all the millions of other iterations of subjectivity and epistemology that are roiling around in the potentialities of philosophical thought every moment.

The admission of the limits of our knowledge as finite creatures is an acknowledgement of the unknown beyond and the ability and invitation to grow into that ever-expanding space of unknowing. The blurring of boundaries and free-flowing through the permeability of knowledge has a

6. Fausto-Sterling, *Sex/Gender*, 10.

7. Barad, "Nature's Queer Performativity," 136.

8. Wesley, *Works* 2:576.

certain queer ring to it. The undefinable, unsolid unknown that we are ever seeking, moving into and out of and into again, fumbling for its zipper in the dark, is a great queer mystery. And the courageous exploration of flirting with this uncertainty is a queer rite of passage. When one is shaped by the ill-fitting ceremonies of heteronormativity, the path to intimacy is not a well-paved thoroughfare, but a self-made trail, forged by hacking down assumptions and requirements with a bravely-wielded machete. As normative forms of intimacy may be unknown to us, in our search for intimacy we become intensely intimate with the unknown.

Being queer in a heteronormative world is like pre-Rosetta-Stone translation, like learning a language from scratch by experience. There's a reason newly out lesbians and gay men are called "gaybies." Like babies, they are learning a whole new culture, a whole new world. From bandana code to fingernail length and a whole self-contained vocabulary of cultural slang, the amount of special knowledge that queers learn is striking, perhaps more so if they come out late into adulthood. Yet they typically face this vast unknown with curiosity and desire that drives them to play, investigate, and learn. These words and worlds can go virtually unnoticed by cisgender heterosexuals in the mainstream of normative society. The unknown modes of queer being—unknown both to cis-heterosexuals and to queers themselves as they grow into their communities—serve the roles of the unknown as Wesley understands them. They engender humility, giving LGBTQ+ people space to grow and revealing a portion of the world where cis-heterosexuals are *not* the norm and do *not* hold the power. They witness to a God who is bigger and more than the cis-heteronoromative hegemony, who seeps into the cracks and the empty spaces of the marginalized, who goes before us as we carve our own path, venturing out away from the safety of society's oppressive norms. They mirror this God who does the selfsame thing. In becoming human, God in Jesus Christ embraces the unknowing of humanity. Jesus himself was a baby, learning language, testing and exploring the unknown. God identifies with our imperfection of knowledge and our queer grappling for understanding as well as intimacy.

An example of Wesley's own imperfection of knowledge is starkly demonstrated in this very sermon. The racist, colonialist examples he provides in considering the question of God's providence to non-European peoples are (or should be) shocking to today's readers. He wonders about God's relation to all the people who live without Christianity, taking the common colonialist assumption that they are less civilized, less intelligent, less capable beings. Of the Pacific Islands, he says, "How little is their state above that of wolves and bears!"[9] He asks about God's care for the "wretched Africans," who are "poor sheep (human if not rational beings!) continually driven to market, and sold like cattle into the vilest bondage."[10] He casts doubt on Peter Kolben and his attempt to "represent [southern Africans] as a respectable people," apparently laughable because of their practice of eating different foods and supposedly engaging in brutal traditions.[11] The American Indians, he asserts, have no religion, no worship, no government, and apparently therefore *that* is why "they are decreasing daily."[12] Of the northern, Indo-Asian others, Wesley says that "to compare them with horses or any of our domestic animals would be doing them too much honour."[13] His ultimate question, considering all of these poor wretches, is that if God so loved and gave his Son for even these, "then why are they thus?"[14] How could it be true that God loved these others and yet lets them live in such pitiable conditions?

It should be clear that Wesley is here affected not only by a simple ignorance, or lack of knowledge of these people all over the world and their cultures and ways of living, but also by an infection of his knowledge and perspective by insidious colonialist-Christian structures of thought.

Historically, the colonialist impulse has always been married to the Christian "missionary" impulse. For example, offers postcolonial feminist theologian Kwok Pui-lan, "in Columbus's journal, the intruders were not described as Spaniards or Europeans, but as Christians, and the Indians were portrayed not as savages, but as people available for conversion."[15] The others, she says, "were deemed as either not fully human or exotic and primitive souls, needing the tutelage of the Man of Reason. Enlightenment thinkers saw that it was the responsibility of the West to bring the benefits of their scientific mind-set and Western civilization to the colonized, to enhance the latter's freedom."[16] Even two-hundred years after Columbus, we can see the same colonialist mindset still active in Wesley's words about

---

9. Wesley, *Works* 2:579.

10. Wesley, *Works* 2:579.

11. Wesley, *Works* 2:579.

12. Wesley, *Works* 2:580.

13. Wesley, *Works* 2:581.

14. Wesley, *Works* 2:581.

15. Kwok, *Postcolonial Imagination and Feminist Theology*, 14.

16. Kwok, *Postcolonial Imagination and Feminist Theology*, 17.

non-Europeans. And, of course, and unfortunately, this mindset is still active in today's Western Christian hegemony.

What's more, the colonial drive of conquest and submission has always included gendered and sexual components. The restriction of both indigenous gender roles and sexual practices, as well as specific violence toward women, were hallmarks of the colonial project. The sexual norms of European Christianity were pushed onto the colonized as "civilization." The colonizers asserted their dominance over tribes and peoples by raping their women, violating both those women's own personhood as well as the sovereignty of the native people. Kwok quotes Andrea Smith saying that "the struggle for sovereignty of Native peoples cannot be separated from the struggle against sexual violence."[17] The colonialist mindset apparent in Wesley's description of other peoples has at its core an oppressive view of gender and sexuality that is ultimately against the perfect love of God and neighbor Wesley touts as holiness.

In the first chapters of Kelly Brown Douglas's classic work *Sexuality and the Black Church*, she traces the Christian colonialist influence on the sexuality of enslaved Africans and their descendants. She discusses "white people's fascination with, yet fear of" black sexuality, explaining that "white culture regards Black men and women as highly sexualized, lascivious beings," and that this colonialist narrative has resulted in the continual repression of black sexualities as a key part of black oppression. As white Europeans infiltrated the African continent, their fascination with and fear of these different-looking bodies birthed and perpetuated myths like we see in Wesley's sermon. These myths dehumanized Africans, which offered justification for their enslavement. "The exploitation of Black sexuality is inevitable and, in fact," she says, "essential for white culture as it serves to nurture white patriarchal hegemony."[18] Control of sexuality is an inherent part of colonialism, and Christianity's involvement in Europe's mission for world domination paired its own religious moralism with racism and misogyny to exert unyielding power over the lives of millions of non-European victims. Douglas quotes Carter Heyward's description of Christianity as "the chief architect of an attitude toward sexuality during the last seventeen-hundred years of European and Euroamerican history—an obsessive, proscriptive attitude."[19] This attitude affected not only practicing

17. Kwok, *Postcolonial Imagination and Feminist Theology*, 15.

18. Douglas, *Sexuality and the Black Church*, 12.

19. Douglas, *Sexuality and the Black* Church, 23.

Christians themselves, but also any of those peoples unlucky enough to fall in the crosshairs of the Christian colonizing empire. Colonizers used this control of sexuality to control those they conquered. Douglas brings in Foucaultian analysis to discuss sexuality's role in maintaining power. "Sexuality is a mechanism by which distinctions can be made between classes and groups of people," she says, and "to question or impugn the sexuality of another bolsters one's own claims to superiority as it suggests another group's inferiority."[20] The colonizers question and malign their victims' sexuality as well as their gender. Any account of the conquer of native peoples of the Americas, for example, will include the rape, if not also the murder, of the nations' women. Douglas shows how the same was the case for the enslaved Africans and the resultant effects on Black sexuality. "Vulnerable to both the racist and sexist ideologies of White culture," Douglas says, "Black women provide the gateway for the White cultural assault on Black sexuality."[21] Black women were property, and the myths and realities of their sexual lives were controlled by white men in the service of propping up the white Christian patriarchy. Even to this day, Douglas argues, "the manner in which Black women are treated in many Black churches reflects the Western Christian tradition's notion of women as evil and its notions of Black women as Jezebels and seducers of men."[22] The control of peoples' gender and sexuality in the service of white Christian colonialism is insidious. Power over a people means sexual power over a people. Sexuality and gender are integral to power, as power is exerted through the regulation of bodies.[23] The intimate link between the two means we cannot hear Wesley's colonialist language and fail to discern the sexualized, racialized bodies beneath.

The white, modernist, Newtonian European way of seeing the world is not the only way. It cannot answer all the many questions of existence and it should not impose itself as the definitive perspective for all people in every place and time. The diversity of human experience is a gift.

Ultimately, when we know better, we should do better. Wesley was no champion of the *status quo*, but rather pushed toward betterment in all areas of his own life and the world. He would contend that we adjust our beliefs and behaviors accordingly as we learn. His focus on progress is

20. Douglas, *Sexuality and the Black Church*, 22.

21. Douglas, *Sexuality and the Black Church*, 36.

22. Douglas, *Sexuality and the Black Church*, 83.

23. Douglas, *Sexuality and the Black Church*, 22.

evident in his discipline and pursuit of holiness, and also in his study and application of medicine and medical procedures, as well as his advocacy for the poor. In this sense, a Wesleyan tradition should always be looking forward. Our acknowledgement of our ignorance should drive us to gain knowledge, and to put that knowledge to work toward a better and more loving existence. A Wesleyan tradition should be a movement into the future, rather than a static institution or a grasping for the past. Because of the imperfection of our knowledge, we are always on the move. We cannot settle into certainty. We follow our desire for knowledge, which leads to fuller understanding and results in the alteration of our path until we learn more and alter it again.

Our ignorance should lead us to curiosity, to wonder, to humility. The perpetual imperfection of our knowledge means we always have the capacity to learn more, to have our minds changed, to experience another way of seeing reality. From different peoples and cultures to our very own insides, the breadth and depth of the potential knowledge to be gained are endless.

Though not without their serious issues, Wesley's questions about God's providence in other places of the world and among different peoples show that our ignorance of others' experiences with God does not mean God is not working there. As God declares through the prophet Isaiah, "My thoughts are not your thoughts, neither are your ways my ways" (Isa 55:8). The ways of God and the universe will always be just outside our grasp. However, this is not a cause for despair but for rejoicing. The queer mystery of all things is expressed in our lives in myriad ways, and we are invited to experience the fullness of reality, not cower from it or staunch its flow. Wesley poses question after question in this sermon, not because he is demanding answers to close a case, but because he is inspired to lean into the queerness of existence—a reality that does not abide by the strict boundaries and categories of modernist thought but is flexible and fluid and resists containment.

The queering of knowledge through history, the upending of previously assumed norms in the light of new information, pushes us toward change. The imperfection of our knowledge entails the imperfection of our tradition. In this case, by *imperfection* I mean *incompleteness*, and the vacuum longs to be filled. The knowledge we gain as we learn can always fill out, or even supplant, our old ways of doing things. In the Wesleyan churches, the knowledge we gain by listening to queer experience and acknowledging the inherent shiftiness of knowledge and experience itself should result in a new way of being, an evolution of tradition. When we face the queer unknown with curiosity rather than fear, with openness rather than resistance, we may be surprised by the ways God works and by the love and grace that is revealed to us in the blessing of our ignorance.

THE GENERAL DELIVERANCE

One of John Wesley's most well-known sermons, the 1782 "The General Deliverance," lays out Wesley's conviction of God's planned redemption of the entire cosmos to a state that, as Albert Outler explains, "may well enhance the status and glory of all creatures above their originals."[1] The sermon has three sections, which move from the prelapsarian paradise, to the current sinful state of nature, and finally to the "manifestation of the children of God" when all things will be made new.

My queer reading of "The General Deliverance" focuses on pleasure. Wesley highlights pleasure as an aspect of the initial perfected state of creation—for humans and non-humans alike—and so I propose that practicing pleasure, in its myriad forms and occasions, can be part of practicing holiness as Christians. The unruly erotic pleasure of queer desire, when acknowledged, honored, and engaged, can lead us toward an embodied, holistic holiness that is indeed very good.

In the first section of this sermon, Wesley takes up the question, "What was the original state of the brute creation?"[2] He explores the nature of the creation before the Fall in its glory and perfection, outlining the natural image of God in humanity that consisted in the principles of self-motion, understanding, will, and liberty. In this uncorrupted state, humanity enjoyed the perfection of these faculties in a way that we today may only experience partially due to the sin in the world. Wesley believes the original state of creation in its perfection can give hints of what is to come in the redeemed Kingdom of God, which, as Jesus told us, is yet at hand. For the promise of God is not simple restoration but renewal, not renovation but transformation.

---

1. Outler, "General Deliverance," in Wesley, *Works* 2:436.
2. Wesley, *Works* 2:438.

A perhaps surprising aspect of Wesley's explication of this perfect state of humanity and the rest of creation is his emphasis on pleasure. In fact, pleasure seems to be an integral part of what it means to be a perfect creation. Happiness, pleasure, and joy are the chief descriptors of the state of first humanity. The first human's perfection of self-motion, understanding, will, and liberty resulted in a perfect state of being, from which their "happiness naturally flowed."[3] And this perfect, innate happiness was actually able to be *increased* by pleasure affected externally.

Wesley says the first human "saw with unspeakable pleasure the order, the beauty, the harmony of all the creatures: of all animated, all inanimate nature."[4] The sensual experience of the materiality of the earth increased the first human's pleasure. Wesley provides a litany of the sensuality of pleasure-making nature: "the serenity of the skies, the sun walking in brightness, the sweetly variegated clothing of the earth; the trees, the fruits, the flowers, 'and liquid lapse of murmuring streams.'"[5] The anthropomorphizing of nature here stresses that pleasure is an embodied, sensual experience. Wesley appeals to all the senses. The sky is serene as an eye fluttering closed or a deep, full breath of fresh air. The sun walks, warm and bright, feeling the stretch and contraction of muscles moving and feet planted on the ground. The earth wears clothing, perhaps striped and silken, smooth and many-colored. The trees sway in a cool breeze. The fruits burst with flavor and juice that runs down the chin and stains the tongue and lips red. The flowers are beautiful and strange-looking and sweet-smelling and pop up where they will. The streams murmur, whispering secrets if one would just listen closely and hear what they have to say. All of these pleasures of nature are to be seen, heard, felt, tasted, smelled. The body is where pleasure plays.

In Wesley's other foundational work, *A Plain Account of Christian Perfection*, he discusses the function of pleasure in the pursuit of Christian perfection. He addresses the question of pleasure, specifically of food but also in general. He asserts that those who are of pure heart, living in perfect love of God and neighbor, "may use pleasing food, without the danger which attends those who are not saved from sin."[6] Holy pleasure can actually be a conduit of God's grace rather than a threat of impertinence or unholiness for those who are dedicated to a life of holiness. Indeed, Wesley

---

3. Wesley, *Works* 2:439.

4. Wesley, *Works* 2:439.

5. Wesley, *Works* 2:439–40. Wesley here quotes John Milton's *Paradise Lost*.

6. Wesley, *Works* 13:172.

says, if one is called to something such as "marriage or worldly business," perhaps here we would well include the experience of sex, "he would be *more capable than ever*; as being able to do all things without hurry or carefulness, without any distraction of spirit."[7] It is clear then in Wesley's thinking that pleasure and perfection are utterly compatible. Wesley says a perfected Christian "may smell to a flower, or eat a bunch of grapes, or take any other pleasure which does not lessen but increase his delight in God."[8] We can surely liken sexual and bodily pleasure to that of smelling flowers and eating grapes. The warm ocean breeze and summer afternoon light coming through the window while looking into the eyes of your lover. All of these can be constructive in the journey of sanctification and experience of Christian perfection.

Wesley says that this first human's pleasure and joy were completely pure, with "no alloy of sorrow or pain," and "nor was this pleasure interrupted by evil of any kind."[9] In their perfection, they experienced perfect and complete pleasure—which would have been grounded in their body— and it was very good. Both humans and creatures experienced pure pleasure by design. "They were all surrounded not only with plenteous food, but with everything that could give them pleasure; pleasure unmixed with pain; for pain was not yet."[10] Having *everything* provided *for their pleasure* was a standard feature of the perfection of Eden. This link between perfection and pleasure is worth exploring, not least because of Protestant Christianity's general aversion to pleasure and Wesley's specific uneasiness about the corrupting potential of pleasure. But what about pleasure's sanctifying potential?

As noted by Wesley himself, the variety of pleasures is vast. The number of ways to make our bodies feel good and blissful and joyous is impossible to count. Sexual pleasure, then, is one kind among many. To think about the queer power of pleasure, we must talk about sexual pleasure, of course, but certainly not exclusively that. And even when discussing sexual pleasure, we must not fall into the heteronormative trap of privileging the genital, the phallic, the outward or productive orgasmic. We must not neglect the subtle titillation of breath on the neck, the trickle of sweat down the spine, the grip of hand on hip. The queer power of the erogenous zones

7. Wesley, *Works* 13:173, emphasis mine.

8. Wesley, *Works* 13:173.

9. Wesley, *Works* 2:440.

10. Wesley, *Works* 2:441.

to create and sustain the kind of unspeakable and uncontrollable pleasure that stems straight from paradise. As religious studies scholar and feminist theologian Margaret Kamitsuka points out, "Focusing too narrowly on orgasmic pleasure may marginalize other pleasures and other bodies."[11] She goes on to say that "once we open the door into forms of sexual pleasure that are not exclusively or even predominantly genitally orgasmic, a number of sexualities, sexual bodies, and sexual practices become topics of inquiry."[12] The queer agenda is always to encourage this opening up, this explosion, this extension and expansion. What else is out there beyond the settled, the structured, the expected, the prescribed?

In her essay on sexual pleasure, Kamitsuka cites progressive religious scholars such as Marvin Ellison and Marcella Althaus-Reid and their work to show that "sexual pleasure is more than just enjoyment; it can be ethically productive and socially transformative."[13] She says that a particular focus on the sexual pleasure of women, which has historically been neglected, can lay the foundation for a more tender, caring, and egalitarian society. She names Catholic theologian Patricia Beattie Jung and her call for "recognizing women's sexual delight as a moral good that awakens self-worth and awareness of the worth of others."[14] The attention to pleasure—especially pleasure beyond the male, genital, orgasmic pleasure—results in a keener awareness of pain as well, and a movement away from the violence that often marks sexual encounters in our culture of compulsory heterosexuality.

Pleasure goes hand in glove with the erotic. The generative power of eroticism is at root a yearning for the pleasure of creation. And it is not merely constructive creation, but it is also the unleashing of that self-shattering nature of pleasure from which bursts forth reality and experience. Philosopher George Bataille says that "the whole business of eroticism is to destroy the self-contained character of the participators as they are in their normal lives."[15] Again we find that the line between pleasure and pain, creation and destruction, life and death, is quite thin. Bataille goes on to say that "erotic activity, by dissolving the separate beings that participate in it, reveals their fundamental continuity, like the

11. Kamitsuka, "Sexual Pleasure," 513.

12. Kamitsuka, "Sexual Pleasure," 514.

13. Kamitsuka, "Sexual Pleasure," 513.

14. Kamitsuka, "Sexual Pleasure," 511.

15. Bataille, *Erotism*, 17.

waves of a stormy sea."[16] The relational power of the erotic lays bare our permeabilities, emphasizing the deep interwovenness of humanity and all creation.

In her book, *The Power of Erotic Celibacy*, Lisa Isherwood says that "it is the erotic that assents to life even in the face of death; the erotic that is a psychological quest for life beyond the bounds of the merely reproductive."[17] The queer impetus of the erotic is pleasure, which may be divorced from reproduction but is nonetheless *always* productive in its own way. Isherwood argues that contrary to some mistaken assumptions of the celibate (or perhaps also the asexual) as devoid of eroticism or pleasure, in truth they can be intimately connected to a deep well of erotic power. We must explode these categories that privilege heterosexual, monogamous formulations of the erotic, that deny the abundant richness and diversity of pleasure and erotic power that bubble up in all kinds of places and faces.

Audre Lorde's essay, "Uses of the Erotic," also emphasizes the wide applicability of the erotic, noting that "we are taught to separate the erotic demand from most vital areas of our lives other than sex."[18] We can understand the connection of the erotic with sex, but we are hesitant to explore how it can birth the creative power of desire in other situations. Because of its chaos, its uncontrollability, its thin line from pain, we fear summoning the erotic power of pleasure into spaces beyond the bedroom. But Lorde says that the erotic is the bridge which connects the spiritual and the political.[19] It is the knowledge in our bodies that can be tapped into at any time and in any setting. It is "a resource within each of us that lies in a deeply female and spiritual plane, firmly rooted in the power of our unexpressed or unrecognized feeling."[20] Again we see the importance of this nebulous unknown inside of us, the space beyond the threshold where we dissolve into pleasure or pain and find the raw ineffable energy of being human.

In the second section of the sermon, Wesley laments the current state of nature and humanity and their corruption and suffering as a result of sin. The pleasure that marked existence in paradise is traded for pain. Not only have creatures become ugly—"terrible and grisly to look upon"[21]—but

16. Bataille, *Erotism*, 22.

17. Isherwood, *Power of Erotic Celibacy*, 93.

18. Lorde, "Uses of the Erotic," 55.

19. Lorde, "Uses of the Erotic," 56.

20. Lorde, "Uses of the Erotic," 53.

21. Wesley, *Works* 2:444.

they are made uglier by their pain. Here perhaps we can question Wesley's sense of "ugliness." At the variety and diversity of creatures' appearances, he experiences fear and disgust rather than pleasure, and this brings to the fore the subjective nature of pleasure. In other words, Wesley assumes an objective aesthetic that aligns with his understanding of the original creation's beauty and pleasure, such that what he finds to be ugly or distasteful in the world must be a result of the Fall.

Pain is also subjective, and here we may also want to consider the interplay of pain and pleasure. In his classic essay, "Is the Rectum a Grave?," queer theorist Leo Bersani describes Freud's speculation "that sexual pleasure occurs whenever a certain threshold of intensity is reached, when the organization of the self is momentarily disturbed by sensations or affective processes somehow 'beyond' those connected with psychic organization."[22] He goes on to say that "the sexual emerges as the *jouissance* of exploded limits, as the ecstatic suffering into which the human organism momentarily plunges when it is 'pressed' beyond a certain threshold of endurance."[23] The concept of *jouissance* is important in both feminist and queer theory. English translators often render the French word as "enjoyment," but just as often provide the caveat that it is more than simply that. In the work of psychoanalyst Jacques Lacan, the subject encounters *jouissance* "in the guises of what might be labeled 'limit experiences,' namely, encounters with that which is annihilating, inassimilable, overwhelming, traumatic, or unbearable. Similarly, *jouissance*, in this vein, is related to transgressive violations, the breaching of boundaries and breaking of barriers."[24] Both pleasure and pain result from this loss of self, or what Bersani calls "self-shattering." In both experiences, we approach our personal limit and then lose ourselves to it. These limit experiences tread tantalizingly on the line between pain and pleasure, the fear of the one exaggerating the thrill of delight of the other. We can think of the arousal produced by a bite, a pinch, a scratch, or that moment when gentle lovemaking escalates to passionate, hungry fucking.[25] The points at which we lose ourselves in the pleasures of sex are

22. Bersani, "Is the Rectum a Grave?," 217.

23. Bersani, "Is the Rectum a Grave?," 217.

24. *Stanford Encyclopedia of Philosophy*, s.v. "Jacques Lacan."

25. The shift from wholesome or sanitized descriptions of sex to more provocative or profane language is an important and necessary shift emphasized especially by Marcella Althaus-Reid and her "Indecent Theology." As Rosemary Radford Ruether says in her essay in honor of Althaus-Reid, "Marcella taught us that to speak truth we must learn to 'talk dirty', to strip off the false modesty that fears to name the realities that are

complex and hazy and beyond our conscious, rational minds—giving rise to the deep inchoate erotic.

It is here that the sexual experiences of BDSM—bondage, domination, sadism, and masochism—may have some important insights to the perfection of pleasure and the pleasure of perfection.[26] Each of these elements of kink involve the interaction between pleasure and pain, but also a very conscious, communicative, and collaborative exploration of those limits. Theologian Lea D. Brown writes in her essay in honor of Marcella Althaus-Reid of queer people of faith, herself included, who "gleefully put their hands under the skirts of God," a phrase used by Althaus-Reid, "by celebrating and trusting in their lived SM [sado-masochist] and Ds [dominant-submissive] experience as both a gift and spiritual blessing in their lives."[27] Brown describes SM and Ds play as necessarily mutual, consenting, and pleasurable for all parties, and highlights that "consent is the one characteristic that defines SM and Ds and sets both apart from abusive, violent or oppressive behaviour."[28] The link of pleasure and pain in this experience is reliant upon desire for pain that results in pleasure. It is an exploration of the power differential and pain potential of the sexual encounter. The varieties of BDSM play consciously face and flirt with the limits of pain and pleasure that beckon us to the ecstatic, erotic oblivion. Further, the use of the word "play" to describe this kind of sexual activity is important, because it signals both the pleasure and joy at work, and also the dimension of and possibility for learning and growth. Play can be salutary in that it gives us low-stakes practice to become the kinds of people we want to be, doing the kinds of things we want to do. We play at holiness; we practice holiness. Brown says that in engaging with the erotic power of SM and Ds, "we are creating liberation for ourselves and our play partners, and we are embracing our power to bring unconditional love and liberation from

---

going on beneath our cover-ups, to recognize and 'undress' the sexual ideologies lurking underneath the systems of domination that impoverish us all." Ruether, "Talking Dirty, Speaking Truth," 267.

26. There is considerable debate about whether kink generally, or particularly BDSM, is to be considered "queer," given its presence in heterosexual experience. However, kink and BDSM play a major role in the LGBTQ+ community because of its similarly questioned and marginalized status in the normative culture. For the purposes of this chapter, I will suspend explicit judgment on this question, but will consider the queerness of kink and BDSM in light of its part in the queer experience.

27. Brown, "Dancing in the Eros of Domination and Submission," 142.

28. Brown, "Dancing in the Eros of Domination and Submission," 145–46.

shame into the world."[29] The movement toward pleasure is the movement toward the perfection of liberation that humanity and creation experienced in the Garden.

Perhaps it is the thin line between pleasure and pain which has tainted our appreciation of pleasure. There is a very real sense in which pleasure is frightening. It is dangerous. It entails a loss of the rationality and reason that the Western Enlightenment has convinced us is the pinnacle of goodness. But the queer claiming of pleasure embraces this risk. It allows us to release the stranglehold on rational moderation to plunge into the self-shattering abyss, beyond our limits of consciousness and control, to the unknown expanse of real experience in which we can explore and feel and create outside the boundaries. The queer experience favors relationality over rationality. And in relationality is always inherently a measure of risk, given the interplay of human beings and our infirmities. As Kamitsuka points out, "human sexual intimacy can be a site of great pleasure and also of anxiety, betrayal, heartbreak, exploitation, and many other painful experiences."[30] Pleasure and pain are intimately connected. For this reason, sexual pleasure can be particularly fraught, especially for those of us who have experienced sexual violence, abuse, and trauma. The connection of sexual pleasure and pain is also especially sensitive to queer folks, who have experienced the pain of spiritual condemnation, familial rejection, and physical violence as a result of the pathologizing of their sexuality and the activities or genders that bring them pleasure. The psychological torment wrought on queer people can have a negative effect not only on their mental health generally, but also on their experience of sexual pleasure. Rather than experiencing pleasure unalloyed with sorrow or pain, as Wesley says, the existence of sin means our experience of pleasure is mingled with guilt, shame, anxiety, and grief.

The sins of humanity—both our individual harms and failings and the broader systemic ills wrought by humans—have a ripple effect on people, creatures, and the environment. "Pain of various kinds, weakness, sickness, diseases innumerable, come upon them," Wesley says, "perhaps from within, perhaps from one another, perhaps from the inclemency of seasons, from fire, hail, snow, or storm, or from a thousand causes which they

29. Brown, "Dancing in the Eros of Domination and Submission," 152.
30. Kamitsuka, "Sexual Pleasure," 517.

cannot foresee or prevent."[31] All of the sensuous sites of pleasure—internal, relational, natural—have become occasions for pain.

With the entrance of sin into the world came pain: that which was purely pleasurable gained a shadow side of "pain and ten thousand sufferings."[32] Wesley says that pain and suffering includes "all those irregular passions, all those unlovely tempers (which in men are sins, and even in the brutes are sources of misery) 'passed upon all' the inhabitants of the earth, and remain in all, except the children of God."[33] All creation experiences pain and suffering as a result of sin. However, these sufferings do not remain in the children of God. The children of God especially should reject pain and harm whenever possible, choosing love in all its forms and manifestations. The children of God are not beholden to suffering but are enjoined to participate in, practice, and play at the eschatological fulfillment of the Kingdom of God, which entails the renewal of perfect pleasure.

The third section of the sermon discusses the restoration and recompense imparted on the "brute creation" in the final day. Wesley is adamant that all creatures "shall be delivered (not by annihilation: annihilation is not deliverance) from the present bondage of corruption into a measure of the glorious liberty of the children of God."[34] All of creation has experienced the pain and suffering of unperfected life in this world, and so much of it not of any fault of our own. And so all of creation groans together, awaiting the birth of a new kind of world.

However, though he stresses the place of and care for all God's creatures in God's age to come, Wesley draws a firm delineation between humanity and the non-human animate creatures. "God regards his meanest creatures much," he says, "but he regards man much more."[35] Wesley subscribes to the Platonic Great Chain of Being, which assigns all of creation to a hierarchy at which God is the top, then angels, then humans, then animals, then plants. Each step up the hierarchy increases the being's faculties, such that, as Wesley explains, brute creation has its own degree of self-motion, understanding, will, and liberty, but that degree is significantly lower than that of human beings. Additionally, humanity is specially able to love and obey God. Wesley explains that this is "the barrier between men

31. Wesley, *Works* 2:444.

32. Wesley, *Works* 2:444.

33. Wesley, *Works* 2:444.

34. Wesley, *Works* 2:445.

35. Wesley, *Works* 2:447.

and brutes": that "man is capable of God; the inferior creatures are not."[36] And therefore "man was the channel of conveyance between his Creator and the whole brute creation."[37] Wesley says humanity was the conduit of God's grace to the rest of creation since humanity was closer to God in the Chain of Being and made in God's image. This image of God was corrupted and the conduit was cut off, causing all of creation to suffer the loss of connection with God. Nature became subject to sorrow and pain because it was subject to humanity; humanity became a conduit for sorrow and pain instead of grace and love.

Queer theory takes issue with this stark demarcation between culture (or humanity) and nature. The distinction itself is artificial as well as vulnerable to manipulation and instability. Thinkers must work overtime to keep the permeable lines from leaking and the structures from crumbling. For one thing, the binary has typically been applied to gender such that men take the place of culture, reason, and rationality, relegating women to the lower order of nature, sensuousness, and emotion.

What's more, as feminist philosopher of science Karen Barad explains, "moralism fashions humans as the only moral agents on the scene, the nature/culture divide is not just any old boundary but the very air it breathes. It's no wonder then that moralism sees itself as duty-bound to protect this sacred boundary with the utmost ferocity."[38] Wesley says exactly as much: the creatures "could not sin, for they were not moral agents."[39] This separation of humanity from the rest of creation causes all kinds of logical and ethical problems, not to mention the queerness that arises when we interrogate the dichotomy closely. Barad summarizes the issue in this way: "If the moral injunction is against 'unnatural' human behaviors, including acting like a beast, then this is because one is acting like nature—performing 'natural' acts."[40] So the so-called "crime against nature" of gay sex assumes the participants are acting like beasts—or as less than their humanity in the chain of being—but indeed the beasts *are* nature. So how could acting like nature be against nature? And how could it be a crime? "What kinds of acts against nature inspire moral outrage?" Barad asks rhetorically, and answers,

---

36. Wesley, *Works* 2:441.

37. Wesley, *Works* 2:440.

38. Barad, "Nature's Queer Performativity," 28.

39. Wesley, *Works* 2:449.

40. Barad, "Nature's Queer Performativity," 29.

"Queer pleasures, for sure."[41] Indeed, humanity is "always already a part of nature, of all manner of beings that the category 'acts against nature' claims to save or defend but in reality erases and demonizes."[42] And the pleasures that are heedless of these false categories may actually be closer to the perfection of the initial creation than to the crime of sin. As queer theologian Jay Emerson Johnson says, "bodily joy might actually constitute a Christian spiritual practice."[43] We might consider engagement in true, holy pleasure as a practice of the perfection that humanity and creation once enjoyed. In the same way we encourage the inbreaking of the not-yet Kingdom of God into the here and now already, we can experience that manifestation in our lives in the form of ecstatic bodily pleasure. We see glimpses of Wesleyan Christian Perfection when we embody perfect love of God and neighbor—and as we have seen in this queer reading, pleasure can be part and parcel of that perfection.

Ultimately, God intends and desires creation's pleasure. Wesley says God is "rich in mercy towards all," God "does not overlook or despise any of the works of his own hands," and God "wills even the meanest of [creatures] to be happy according to their degree."[44] Pleasure is the result of the individual's alignment with perfection. In the story of pre-Fall creation, humanity lived in perfect love of God and non-human neighbor, and likewise experienced holy harmony of erotic power and pleasure. The co-creative force and deep body knowledge of the erotic were unblemished and unrestricted, readily accessible and put to use in such a way that the result was perfect happiness and pleasure. As children of God today, we should focus our practice of holiness in part on the reclamation of that perfect pleasure—including the perfect pleasure in the erotic experiences of our bodies.

41. Barad, "Nature's Queer Performativity," 30.

42. Barad, "Nature's Queer Performativity," 33.

43. Johnson, Peculiar Faith, 88.

44. Wesley, Works 2:438.

ON THE WEDDING GARMENT

If the clothes make the man, then queer theory is the child pointing out that the emperor isn't wearing any. Our heteronormative, patriarchal society is the trickster who convinces us there's something there when there's not—and we continue to act as if there is. Few things do more to reinforce gender roles and expectations than the clothing we wear. And while fashion and standards of decorum have changed through time and culture, clothing remains an important signal we use to express our gender, whether to abide by the normative bounds or to resist them.

In his sermon, "On the Wedding Garment," Wesley takes as his text Matthew 22, the parable of the wedding banquet, which culminates in a question of clothing and its symbolic value. In this parable, a king prepares a wedding banquet for his son, but those whom he invites refuse to come. So instead, the king instructs his servants to invite anyone they can find from the streets. But when the king comes in to see this rabble of guests, he sees one who is not wearing the proper wedding attire, and he has the man bound and cast out into the darkness.

Traditional readings of this parable type the king as God the Father and the son as Christ, God's Son. The wedding feast, then, is the church—a gathering in celebration of the king's son. People are invited in, and some refuse. The people who do attend the banquet are held to certain expectations of appropriate dress.

As the people were invited to the banquet, it was not made explicit that there was a dress code. Certainly one can assume that knowledge of the appropriate clothing would be obvious. Given the cultural norms of the time, the people invited would know the proper garments to wear. However, if that were the case, we might wonder why a person would even bother to show up dressed inappropriately. If everyone already implicitly knew to wear the proper wedding garments, it would be particularly foolish to knowingly show up without one. The man was speechless when confronted about his clothes, suggesting he had no answer for why he was let in without the clothes, or why he was not wearing them in the first place. Did he not know about the proper dress? Did he not own such clothing? Could he not afford it? In the ancient world, having multiple sets of clothing would be a significant expense not available to every person. Did he think he could attend the banquet unnoticed? Perhaps he was simply stunned, having been invited in only to be questioned and then sent out for no real fault of his own.

The silence of those who have been cast out is deafening. Queer reading asks us to interrogate these gaps and silences we find in Scripture's stories. Surely this man has his own version of events. Surely his choice of dress was not made out of malice. Surely he was trying to please the king, whose capricious invitation caught the man unawares.

The king seems to have a lot of trouble creating the kind of banquet he wants. We might wonder why the initial invitees refused to attend, and why some of them had such a violent reaction to their invitation. When the king retaliates by destroying these invitees' cities, we see that perhaps this king is not a person one wishes to celebrate with, though neither is he someone to cross. The parable does not necessarily cast the king in a good light. He razes cities and casts out his invited guests. He was angry that people did not want to attend his banquet, and then capriciously sends away one of those who did come. Is this king supposed to represent God? Is this the kind of God we want to worship? Is this a faithful portrayal of a God of love and justice? Wesley's questioning of others' interpretations of the parable invites us to question them as well. Perhaps there are other, more fruitful ways of reading it. Reading this story through a queer lens allows us to question this image of God as an angry king—the image we are given is one of a powerful, impulsive patriarch. It's the image of the oppressive heteronormative hegemony we are so familiar with. We might wonder what the king is actually wearing. Does *he* have the appropriate wedding garment for the supper of the Lamb? Or does the emperor have no clothes?

Verse 10 says that the bad as well as the good were gathered into the banquet hall. It's worth noting that the man without the wedding clothes is not identified either as one of the good or one of the bad. His moral character had no bearing on whether or not he belonged there; rather, it was his appearance. His ability to conform to the community, to fit the setting and the expectations of the host, the one in power, was the deciding factor of whether he belonged. He has no voice to plead his case.

In the end, to name this parable and subsequently Wesley's sermon "On the Wedding Garment" is to reify an absence. The central figure of the text—the garment—is nowhere to be seen, but and therefore is of the utmost importance. The lack of this garment makes it ever more present in the meaning of the story. What is this garment? Is it an illusion of some traveling tricksters or a symbolic acquiescence to the whims of a king? Is it expensive *haute couture* or the product of homegrown stitchery? Will it go day to night? Can we wear it to church and the gay bar?

Wesley begins his sermon on this parable by identifying common errors he finds people committing in their understanding of the passage. Of primary concern is the interpretation of the missing garment itself. He first takes up his quarrel with other interpreters and preachers of the text, who have taken the wedding garment to signify the proper receiving of eucharist. He makes clear his belief that this parable is not about the Lord's Supper, and that "probably we should never have imagined it, but that the word 'supper' occurred therein."[1] Wesley then considers those who have interpreted the wedding garment as the righteousness of Christ, since that is what is required to appear before God. He reasons that this can't be it either, because if Christ's righteousness is sufficient for all people, then how could some be found not to be clothed in it? Therefore, cross referencing Hebrews 12:14, Wesley contends that the wedding garment must signify "the holiness without which no man shall see the lord."[2] He says that the righteousness of Christ, indeed necessary "for any soul that enters into glory," affords us our *claim* to that glory, whereas holiness testifies to our *fitness* to dwell in such glory.[3] The garment is not what allows the man into the feast, but it is the appropriate garb for the occasion.

So then, what is the holiness that is the appropriate dress for the banquet of the Lamb? "In a word," Wesley says, "holiness is having 'the mind that was in Christ', and the 'walking as Christ walked.'"[4] Wesley describes several ways this holiness has been perverted and disguised, such that Christians will seek other clothes than the proper garment of holiness. First, he describes idolatry—"things prescribed as Christian holiness, although flatly

1. Wesley, *Works* 4:141.
2. Wesley, *Works* 4:144.
3. Wesley, *Works* 4:144.
4. Wesley, *Works* 4:147.

contrary thereto."[5] Among these things he specifically includes Catholic devotion to saints and the Virgin Mary. However, he follows this up with a second thing that is contrary to holiness: persecution. He is adamant that maltreatment of others for differing beliefs cannot be part of the Christian life. He calls out Protestants who may feel superior for not having taken part in the literal Crusades, saying that "doing anything unkind to another for following his own conscience is a species of persecution."[6] And surely Protestants just as well as Catholics are guilty of such persecution. This is of course abundantly true in the case of LGBTQ+ Christians and their experiences with the church. They have suffered extensively from the churches' idolatry and persecution. By placing beliefs and practices as more important than the care and nurture of God's children, churches have made idols of their homophobia and transphobia, and consequently churches have mistreated and oppressed queer people in the name of the very God who loves them. Following one's own conscience and, particularly in the case of committed Christians, following one's leading by the Holy Spirit is typically not a light matter entered into flippantly. To harass or ostracize a person for their honest, good-faith efforts cannot be holiness.

Another perversion of holiness, as Wesley sees it, is "to represent trifles as necessary to salvation."[7] Faith is what is required, and holiness the appropriate garment, but any other thing "not expressly enjoined in the Holy Scripture" is not to be counted as a requirement for salvation.[8] Among such trifles he includes, perhaps surprisingly, *orthodoxy*. Having certain right opinions about God or theology is not a prerequisite for salvation. One needn't have orthodox beliefs to receive the saving grace of God; and having orthodox beliefs will not save a person. In fact, Wesley says, "a man may judge as accurately as the devil, and yet be as wicked as he."[9] Wesley's holiness is not about judgment, rightness, and condemnation, but about embodying the mind of Christ, which is always love. The policing of clothing—and by extension other forms of self- and gender-expression— could similarly be considered such a "trifle." Most Wesleyan churches in the United States tend to present themselves as spaces where people may "come as they are," with clergy and congregants wearing casual clothes on

5. Wesley, *Works* 4:144.
6. Wesley, *Works* 4:146.
7. Wesley, *Works* 4:146.
8. Wesley, *Works* 4:146.
9. Wesley, *Works* 4:146.

Sunday mornings. But at the same time, queer folks who present them-selves unapologetically as such are still likely to be cast out. The United Methodist Book of Discipline states that "self-avowed practicing homosex-uals" are unfit for service to the church.[10] And while there is certainly more to such self-avowal than appearance or clothing choice, such expressions are among the ways queer folks avow themselves and claim their identi-ties—which may include their various genders as well as their attractions to others of their same gender. Since none of this is "expressly enjoined in the Holy Scripture," using clothing or standards of orthodoxy as measure-ments for "holiness" in order to gatekeep and exclude should be considered antithetical to Wesley's vision of holiness.

The culmination of the sermon is this, says Wesley: "The God of love is willing to save all the souls that he has made," however, "he will not force them to accept of it," and ultimately each person must "choose holiness by grace, which is the way, the only way, to everlasting life."[11] Each person may choose to put on the garment of holiness that is offered to them by grace. God in God's love makes available a vast wardrobe from which we can create our own expression of holiness, through works of mercy and piety, through an increasingly perfect love of God and neighbor, and find ourselves dressed—in our own way—as part of the banquet, the church.

To queer this story and this sermon, we can take different routes. Just as we make conscious, critical choices about what to wear and how to present ourselves, we can make conscious, critical choices about how we read the Scriptures. And there are so many choices we can make! On the one hand, we can think about the ways queer folks resist the demand to conform to a heteronormative society and church—they stand out and are kicked out, not to enjoy the wedding and its celebration, even after being forcibly "invited." Though perhaps not wantonly, they simply don't fit, don't belong, and are ushered out. We can see this as an indictment of the vicious and capricious king. The hegemonic ruler of heteropatriarchy just wants things done his way, the way he has decided in his arbitrary univocal power is the proper way. By and large, people show up as asked, as expected, in their cisgender, heterosexual wedding garments without question. But some of us, of no fault of our own, show up queer and pay the price.

On the other hand, we can think about the ways that queer folks have their own systems of normative dress that create community. Though they

10. *Book of Discipline*, ¶ 304.3.
11. Wesley, *Works* 4:148.

may not be in the majority, though they may not be the king's "first choice" of guests, they still create cohesive aesthetic organizations that construct their social spaces.

Queer aesthetics—both in philosophical and literary theory and in personal expression and cultural production—provide a frame for us now to consider the Gospel writer's and Wesley's wedding garment. As an article of clothing, a piece of symbolism, the garment serves as a focal point of individual fitness in a community. Let us consider the queer norms of femme/butch aesthetics in the lesbian/women-loving-women community as an example of the creation of community based on the wearing of particular garments.

Elizabeth Lapovsky Kennedy and Madeline Davis's classic ethnographic work, *Boots of Leather, Slippers of Gold,* gives a thorough overview of the origins and progressive evolution of butch and femme culture in Buffalo, New York, from the 1930s through the 1950s. Kennedy and Davis's in-depth interviews with lesbians engaged in Buffalo's gay bar scene give a window to the burgeoning queer culture before the sexual revolution of the 1960s and 1970s. The basis of the aesthetic was a dichotomy of masculine and feminine, with the butches presenting a masculine appearance and performance and the femmes presenting a feminine one.

The historical development of the butch and femme aesthetics among lesbians tells us a lot about appearance and community building. "The presence of the butch," say Kennedy and Davis, "with her distinctive dress and mannerism, or of the butch-fem couple—two women in a clearly gendered relationship—announced lesbians to one another and to the public."[12] The roles expressed by mid-century lesbians were consciously chosen and performed as part of their mindful experience of gender and sexuality. As socially "deviant," they were not afforded the privilege of falling into roles or clothing accidentally or as a result of simply acquiescing to the norm. Butches and femmes make thoughtful decisions about the clothes they wear and the image they present to the world.

The butch/femme roles were especially important for lesbian culture in the mid-twentieth century. "You had to be [into roles]," one of Kennedy and Davis's subjects explains. "If you weren't, people wouldn't associate with you. . . . You had to be one or the other or you just couldn't hang around."[13]

12. Kennedy and Davis, *Boots of Leather, Slippers of Gold,* 152.
13. Kennedy and Davis, *Boots of Leather, Slippers of Gold,* 166.

The established roles and aesthetics of butch and femme were crucial in the cohesion of the community.

Often, particularly in heterosexual world and third-wave feminist world, lesbian butch/femme relationships are considered an aping of heterosexual roles and relationships. However, as Evelyn Blackwood explains, "butch-femme culture was not an imitation of heterosexuality, but a specifically lesbian culture and lifestyle."[14] Kennedy and Davis also emphasize this point, insisting that butches were not taking on the dress and mannerisms of men to *be like men*, but rather to construct a particular kind of female masculinity.[15] Indeed, in claiming this masculinity, butches claimed a female autonomy of body, gender, and sexuality. Butch lesbians were emphatically *women*, but acting the part—the swaggering, assertive, independent part—typically played by men in heterosexual society. Thereby butches wrenched free of heterosexual roles and hierarchies by claiming the top for themselves.

The masculinity claimed by butch lesbians therefore renders null the masculinity of the cis-hetero patriarch that we see, for example, in the king of the parable. The queer masculine aesthetic points out that the emperor has no clothes. The king's masculinity is parodied and reworked to show a different way of being.

The imitation, then, is actually more like parody. Daniel Williford's work describes the role of parody in queering aesthetics: "When something is an overt construction, transparently false, it becomes the prototype of itself, performing, as it were, its own blueprint."[16] The butch's overt act or performance of masculinity, precisely as a woman, creates entirely new possibilities for masculinity and womanhood itself. In putting on the masculine garment, the butch claims for herself a female autonomy, a female ownership of her own sexuality and personhood. Likewise, the femme is not merely submitting to heterosexual expectations of femininity, but rather engaging in a similar "overt construction," often consciously exaggerating elements of "traditional" femininity in order to demonstrate femmes' claiming it for themselves rather than having it be foisted on them by heteronormative society. As Gaby Sandoval says in her essay "Passing

---

14. Blackwood, "From Butch-Femme to Female Masculinities," 97. This point has been historically and is still today debated in the LGBTQ+ community.

15. Blackwood cites J. Halberstam's work on female masculinities as distinct from male masculinities, accessed in a particular way by butch lesbians.

16. Williford, "Queer Aesthetics."

Loquería," "I choose my femininity; it does not choose me."[17] In fact, Leah Lilith Albrecht-Samarasinha claims in her essay in the same book that "femmes share more with drag queens and MTF transgendered people than we do with straight women. . . . Femme women, like MTFs, construct their girl-ness, and construct it the way it works for us."[18] The queer femme aesthetic is constructed in, by, and for this distinct community.

So much of queer identity is in the conscious claiming of self that is taken for granted and received without question by cis-heterosexuals. It is putting on—or refusing to put on—the "appropriate" garments and playing by the rules or taking the risk of being sent out to the street. While nature-or-nurture and born-this-way arguments are still up for debate, the claiming of queer identity and aesthetics remains a conscious choice, a purposeful performance and expression that queer people navigate in the world on a daily basis. Queer aesthetics can function to signal that one is both a legitimate part of a community and simultaneously apart from another community.

When it comes down to it, the wedding garment is not about a wedding at all. Not the sermon, not the parable, not the garment itself. The bride is nowhere to be found. The desire, the sex, the love is all in the background, and all inaccessible except to those who conform to an unspoken expectation of presentation in the community. Similarly, queerness is not simply about what folks do in their bedrooms. LGBTQ+ life hinges on the experience of community and culture of belonging where one was previously excluded. The interrogation of self and exploration of desire and meaning outside the unquestioned assumptions of hegemonic narratives creates a shared narrative that clothes us in such a way that we can recognize ourselves in each other and coalesce into our own celebratory banquet. Perhaps we can envision a banquet that is not initiated by a murderous, gatekeeping king. Perhaps our banquet does not conscript the unprepared into its number, but stops and reflects when people do not want to join us of their own accord. The socially constructed aesthetics of queer community build something particular and illustrative of the kind of banquet we might hope to see hosted by a God whose nature and name is Love. Such a God values the creative and rebellious ways that queer love emerges and thrives in an oppressive world and an oppressive church. Such a God does not quash life. Such a God does not send the hungry away or despise

17. Sandoval, "Passing Loquería," 172.
18. Albrecht-Samarasinha, "On Being a Bisexual Femme," 141–42.

a broken heart. The queer holiness of LGBTQ+ life reflects this expansive, rule-breaking love.

When we combine Wesley's determination of the wedding garment as symbolic of holiness, and the ability of the LGBTQ+ to construct their own codes of dress, we can start to think of the specific expressions of holiness that queer Christians bring to the wedding banquet of the church. If the garment of holiness is what allows us to see the Lord, then the garment will fit each of us differently. It's not one size fits all. Because the basis of holiness is love, and love is contingent, singular, and situational, personal holiness also will be shaped by the moment, the individual, and the particular grace afforded to the person. Holiness is peculiar—queer—in this way. The holiness we wear will signal our fitness as appropriate, and therefore will be recognizable, but that doesn't mean it will look identical to everyone else's. While there is a kind of cohesion when it comes to, for example, the femme aesthetic, the individual expression of this aesthetic will vary widely from person to person. The femme will nonetheless be recognizable as femme, especially in relation to her butch, but the particulars of what *make* her recognizable as femme will be different from any other femme. Her nails, her hair, her heels, her dress, are all specifically *hers* and cannot be prescribed. John Wesley says that God has prepared the banquet for humanity, but "will not force them to accept of it. He leaves them in the hands of their own counsel."[19] We choose holiness as we choose the clothes we wear.

Wesley says that God cries, "Be holy, and be happy; happy in this world, and happy in the world to come."[20] God desires our holiness, yes, and God also desires our happiness—both of which, by God's grace, are up to us to put on or not. We choose to adorn ourselves in the trappings of the community in which we find belonging. For LGBTQ+ Christians, this means engaging both the aesthetics of our queer family and also the holiness of the church. We might cut our hair a certain way to be recognizable to our queer siblings; and we might engage in works of piety and works of mercy to be recognizable to our Wesleyan siblings. Putting on the garment of the community is an act of choosing. It's an act of claiming for ourselves the happiness and holiness that is available to us, even—perhaps especially—as queer people.

Because LGBTQ+ people have not been able to take our sexuality or our gender for granted, we are practiced in considering the options,

19. Wesley, *Works* 4:148.
20. Wesley, *Works* 4:148.

reading the room, and deciding consciously what we must do for ourselves. Indeed, many queer people spend years agonizing over the garments they should wear, how they should appear to the world that is both acceptable to others and feels true to themselves. And this rigorous self-assessment often does not end with, say, a coming out event or wearing lipstick for the first time. Queer folks are constantly thinking about the way they present themselves, judging their relative safety or their ability to be recognized, regularly wracked with anxiety over the possibility of being cast out into the darkness.

Likewise, holiness is not a garment that might be put on accidentally. Particularly in the Methodist way of John Wesley, it requires a great deal of reflection, discipline, and involvement in community. Wesley's intensive journaling, spiritual practice, and engagement in groups of accountability demonstrate a commitment to the pursuit of holiness that is worth emulating. Queer holiness incorporates all of these aspects into a way of life that is conscious, critical, and aware in a way that comes from having a queer experience of self and society. To be queer in a cis-heteronormative world requires careful contemplation and questioning of ourselves and each other that ultimately dovetails in becoming holy in this same world. In the end, the questions and challenges will always point to love. The powerful, world-wrecking and world-remaking love experienced in queer life is an image of the holy love of God.

Perhaps we can also think of holiness along the lines of queer parodic aesthetics, wherein the love we demonstrate toward our neighbors is the excessive, over-the-top kind of love we see in others of Jesus' parables. The father of the prodigal son throws a party in celebration of his already wasteful child (Luke 15:11–32). The landowner pays a full day's wages to the man who worked in the vineyard only an hour (Matt 20:1–16). This kind of care and celebration of others is just the kind of overt parody that queer aesthetics are made of. The foolishness—indeed, the queerness—of these stories told by Jesus is the model for our expectations of what holiness looks like and how we can recognize the Kingdom of God in the world. The queerness of feeding the poor, visiting the prisoner, welcoming the stranger in a world where these acts of mercy are seen as foolish or even dangerous is, as one might say, *a look*. It's a look that signals to the world that we are Christians, that we endeavor to love our neighbors as God loves them, as God's own children.

ON CHARITY

The Scripture text that is the basis of this sermon deserves to be copied here and read in full:

> Though I speak with the tongues of men and of angels, and have not charity, I am become a sounding brass, or a tinkling cymbal. And though I have the gift of prophecy, and understand all mysteries, and all knowledge; and though I have all faith, so as to remove mountains, and have not charity, I am nothing. And though I bestow all my goods to feed the poor, and give my body to be burned, and have not charity, it profiteth me nothing. (1 Cor 13:1–3 KJV)

Before he embarks on a discussion of what charity is, Wesley himself, as well as Albert Outler in his footnotes to the sermon, discusses briefly the tricky politics of translation. For here in the 1611 King James Version, also known as the Authorized Version, the translators render *agape* as "charity" rather than the "love" that we are more familiar with. Indeed, Wesley says, "It was in an unhappy hour this alteration was made," and "the ill effects of it remain to this day."[1] He especially worries that the connotation of charity as "little more than almsgiving"[2] is a major problem in understanding this passage and the actual wide-ranging definitions and practice of *love*. Translation is such a fraught process. We are right to question and test the ways the Bible is presented to us, particularly to those of us who cannot read its ancient, original languages. Who does the translating, and what are their goals? Who benefits or is disadvantaged by the way certain words are translated? Who is erased? Wesley points out to us that all translation is interpretation. And the way we interpret Scripture matters.

1. Wesley, *Works* 3:294.
2. Wesley, *Works* 3:294.

The biblical texts were written by dozens of people over hundreds of years, millennia ago and miles away. Making any sense of them for today's Christians is no small feat. It's always useful to remember just how queer these texts were, are, and continue to be. That is, the cultures they discuss and stories they tell don't fit neatly into the norms of our society. They come from entirely different circumstances. Their assumptions and prescriptions simply won't map neatly onto today's world. We are constantly translating, interpreting, retranslating, and reinterpreting.

One relevant example of the impact of biblical translation is the introduction of the word "homosexual" to some English versions of the biblical text. There is much debate over some Pauline verses that are often used to condemn contemporary expressions of queer love. For example, the 2001 English Standard Version uses the phrase "men who practice homosexuality" to translate the two Greek words *malakoi* and *arsenokoitai* in 1 Corinthians 6:9, whereas Wesley's King James Version says "effeminate" and "abusers of themselves with mankind." The difference of translation reflects different understandings and attitudes about sexuality that had developed in the three-hundred intervening years.

In his *History of Sexuality*, Michel Foucault analyzes the Victorian "repression" of sexuality as a taboo that actually resulted in the proliferation of sexual language. It had to be defined so that it could be confessed and manipulated. "In the course of recent centuries," Foucault says, sexuality has "multiplied in an explosion of distinct discursivities which took form in demography, biology, medicine, psychiatry, psychology, ethics, pedagogy, and political criticism."[3] Indeed, he says, "this whole thicket of disparate sexualities was labeled," and not simply to "exclude them from reality," but in order to exert a complex of power on society.[4] This power in turn drew out from the commonplace secret the named desires and pleasures of bodies in the Western world.

Dale Martin's essay on the changes in translation of *malakoi* and *arsenokoitai* over time asserts that interpretations of the words "as condemning modern homosexuality have been driven more by ideological interests in marginalizing gay and lesbian people than by the general strictures of historical criticism."[5] Martin provides a thorough analysis of the English translation of these words over time, pointing out the historical contextual

3. Foucault, *History of Sexuality*, 33.

4. Foucault, *History of Sexuality*, 1:41.

5. Martin, "Arsenokoites and Malakos," 117.

use of the words and the contemporary deviation from standard philological practice. Instead of a change in translation based on, say, historical evidence or newly discovered contextual support, it instead "reflected the invention of the category of 'homosexuality' as an abnormal orientation, an invention that occurred in the nineteenth century."[6]

This is a slight digression, but a salubrious one, given the oft-cited argument that the word "homosexual" did not exist in English translations of the biblical texts until 1946.[7] The argument can be taken further to assert that there was no such thing as a "homosexual" before the word was coined in the late-nineteenth century. Our conceptualizations of sexual feelings, acts, and relationships have evolved over time, culture, and language, and this is reflected in our translation and interpretation of the Bible. This fact also helps us think more honestly and critically about the historical milieu in which the Bible was written. We do well to keep in mind that the context of the Bible is not our context, and if its stories strike us as strange it's because *they are*.

The point here is that Wesley understood the vagaries of translation and interpretation, and that it is often, or perhaps always, tricky and unfaithful. He acknowledges the necessity of interpreting what has already been interpreted for us. He acknowledges that our translations and our interpretations of those translations have real consequences for the life of the church. Reading the Bible today, in English, is like playing a convoluted game of telephone. We would do well to keep these complications in mind, eschewing simplistic answers and uncritical certainty. What's more, as Martin quotes Augustine, and as Wesley's sermon also bears out, "Whoever thinks that he understands the divine Scriptures or any part of them so that it does not build the double love of God and of our neighbor does not understand it at all."[8] For a Christian to interpret Scripture to have any other purpose or meaning than love is a grave error. To use the Bible as a weapon to harm God's beloved children rather than as a balm against injustice is a tragic mistake. Love is the end of the Scriptures, the nature of God, and the purpose of this sermon.

6. Martin, "Arsenokoites and Malakos," 118.

7. The initial publication of the Revised Standard Version of the New Testament was the first to translate *malakoi* and *arsenokoites* as "homosexuals" in 1 Cor 6:9. The New Revised Standard Version (1989) renders those words in that verse as "male prostitutes" and "sodomites," respectively.

8. Martin, "Arsenokoites and Malakos," 130. This quote is from Augustine's *Christian Doctrine* 1.35.40.

Wesley says that the love the Apostle Paul speaks of in this passage is the love of neighbor that flows "from that faith which is the operation of God."[9] Consequently, he raises the question of whether true love, and thereby salvation, is possible for those who do not believe in Christ. His answer is this: "'He that believeth not shall be damned,' is spoken of them to whom the gospel is preached. Others it does not concern." Further, he says, "How it will please God, the Judge of all, to deal with them, we may leave to God himself."[10] Wesley releases his audience from the responsibility of forcing others into "salvation." While his evangelical spirit means conversion is his goal, Wesley is not so interested in coercion or reasoning. Rather Wesley preaches the gospel to his fellow Christians as an invitation to the holiness of God that is the experience of God's grace and love, and the outpouring of that grace and love to all the world.

Wesley goes on to describe the characteristics of the love Paul is talking about using the well-known love passage from 1 Corinthians 13. Let us follow his analysis and think about how each aspect of love is embodied in queer experience and relationships. In so doing, we can see the very real and holy nature of queer love, and make plain its importance as an aspect of the church. That is, the church would do well to see queer love as a vital model for loving the world, God, and others.

"First," Wesley begins, "Love is not puffed up."[11] Love is humble. As we have mentioned in other chapters, there is an honesty in humility. A clear-eyed assessment of one's self and others. Queer love especially is based in a humility that respects one another's hard-won identities and struggles. Queer love must be tender in its approach, seeking the truth of each person's desires with care. Intimacy with another queer person, who has likely experienced trauma at the hands of cis-heteropatriarchal society and has likely had to overcome incredible challenges to simply be themselves in the world, is a privilege. It can't be taken for granted and requires humility—never entitlement. Humility entails sober sensitivity to others' identities and experiences. Queer love's humility concedes ignorance and embraces curiosity. Because there is no script, no "right" or "expected" way to love queerly, queer love asks questions without judgement and joyfully explores the other in gratitude. Queer love is a shared experience of vulnerability between people, and there is no space in the vulnerable encounter with the

---

9. Wesley, *Works* 3:295.

10. Wesley, *Works* 3:295–96.

11. Wesley, *Works* 3:296.

other for any airs of superiority. Just honest, open palms and expectant eyes and mouths.

Second, love is not provoked, it is not easily angered.[12] "However provoked," Wesley says, the person who is full of love "does not return evil for evil. . . . Yea, he blesses those that curse him, and does good to them that despitefully use him and persecute him."[13] Queers who love fully and truly, who love themselves and others with purity and passion, no longer have space in their hearts for the anger that returns evil for the evil done to them as a result of their sexuality. Such anger is valid, no doubt. But the preoccupying, all-consuming, reactive anger that is so often the rightful inheritance of those who decide to live true to themselves in spite of the expectations or requirements of their families, churches, or workplaces, can ultimately, through queer love of self and others, and the beauty of queer life, transmute into a holy disinterest. Once a queer person fully embraces their queer love of themselves and others, they can also be freed to bless those who curse them and wish good for those who have persecuted them. This freedom is some of the magic and grace of queer love. The transforming love of God, working in queer ways among queer people, leads to peace, forgiveness, and strength. And this peace, forgiveness, and strength can extend even to those who would make themselves enemies of LGBTQ+ Christians. Queer love frees us from hatred toward those who hate us.

Similarly, and thirdly, love is long-suffering. Wesley says that love "arms the soul with inviolable patience; not harsh, stoical patience, but yielding as the air, which, making no resistance to the stroke, receives no harm thereby."[14] There is so much resistance that LGBTQ+ Christians face in the course of their lives and relationships. It's a gift when their queer love allows them to calm the struggle and release their perceived responsibility to fight in exchange for permission to let go of the strikes leveled against them. When we lean into the queer love of the queer self and others, it becomes easier to bear the barbs of hatred flung our way. We use the strength of love in our queer community to hold us up and keep us going, no matter the hardships we face from an antagonistic society and church. And, as Wesley suggests, the perseverance engendered by queer love is not about

12. Wesley spends some time in this section of the sermon explaining that the "easily" of "easily provoked" or "easily angered" is not an appropriate translation, though it still appears in many versions of the text.

13. Wesley, *Works* 3:298.

14. Wesley, *Works* 3:298.

muscling through, but more like the bracing refreshment of a deep breath of fresh air. The flowing air of queer love enters our bodies, nourishes our cells, and exits again changed and ready to cycle on into the world. This transformative breathing metaphor is reminiscent of the Buddhist practice of *tonglen,* which Christian theologian Sharon Betcher considers christologically in her book *Spirit and the Obligation of Social Flesh.* She describes the practice as a way to connect with and transform distress and grief by "taking in pain and suffering and sending out well-being and happiness," by focusing on "moving breath through the occlusions that suffering brings."[15] We breathe in pain, and breathe out love. It is a transformative practice. Queer love helps us withstand the often unfair challenges we face as queer people by reminding us of our worth, our beauty, and our belonging. We are able to take in the harm sent our way, let the love in our hearts and bodies transform it, and release it back out into the world as strength, joy, and peace. And, as Wesley says referencing Romans 12:20, in doing so, we "heap coals of fire, of melting love, upon [our enemy's] head."[16] As the saying goes, living well is the best revenge.

The special particularity of queer love is apparent in the ways LGBTQ+ people show up for each other in community. From the queer-led groups that formed during the height of the AIDS crisis to fight for treatment and prevention measures and to care for the abandoned sick and dying, to the creation of "chosen families" and mutual aid networks that support diasporic queers estranged from their childhood homes, the love of queer folks is deep and wide and flourishes defiantly in the face of society's attempts to quash it. Queer love also goes far beyond sex, though sex is an important and legitimate facet of creating and expressing it. Queer love shapes and nurtures relationships in creative ways that are based on real needs and lived experience rather than scripts or normative assumptions. Queer love embodies so many of the characteristics that Wesley holds up as emblematic of the true and holy love discussed in the Apostle Paul's letters. As such, we would do well not to discount it wholesale because of its queerness, but rather open ourselves and our churches to see what we might learn about love by loving and being loved by queer folk.

In the short second section of the sermon, Wesley considers several things that often take the place of love in our lives and relationships: eloquence, or "talking well, particularly on religious subjects"; knowledge,

15. Betcher, *Spirit and the Obligation of Social Flesh,* 94.
16. Wesley, *Works* 3:298.

prophecy, and "knowledge of Scripture in particular"; faith; good works; and "suffering for righteousness' sake," even unto death.[17] But all of these things, though good and worth seeking, are nothing without love behind them. "Nothing," he says, "is higher than Christian love—the love of our neighbor flowing from the love of God."[18] How often, truly, do we see these poor substitutions made in exchange for real love toward queer people in our churches! When people think they are "loving the sinner, but hating the sin," or when people believe they are the sole defender of a God whose integrity might be besmirched by the touch of a queer person, or when people think their beliefs are the only correct beliefs, or when people perform perhaps well-intentioned but patronizing evangelism of queer people, the queer people involved are not being *loved*. Wesley is convinced that these are common aspects of "religion improperly so called," as opposed to the proper religion, which is always characterized primarily by love.

In the third and final section of the sermon, Wesley sets out to demonstrate "that neither any one of these five qualifications [eloquence, knowledge, faith, good works, suffering], nor all of them together, will avail anything before God without the love above described."[19] He shows how these particulars of religion improperly so called are none of them sufficient for what he considers the true religion—that which we are called to by God in Christ.

Being able to speak well, having a gift for rhetoric and persuasion, possessing a large platform and much influence, are all often goals of Christian preachers. But there is incredible danger in such things when they are lacking in love. For example, Church Clarity, which is a crowd-sourced database that scores churches based on the clarity or ambiguity of their policies on gendered leadership and LGBTQ+ issues, reported in 2017 that *zero* of the one-hundred largest churches in the United States had affirming LGBTQ+ policies.[20] These one-hundred churches boast a combined attendance of nearly a million members, meaning that every Sunday these million people hear an eloquent word from their charismatic leaders, but without love for their LGBTQ+ neighbors, or even, as the case may be, for themselves.[21] To have this kind of reach, to have so many people hear

17. Wesley, *Works* 3:298–99.

18. Wesley, *Works* 3:300.

19. Wesley, *Works* 3:300.

20. See "Scoring America's 100 Largest Churches for Clarity (2017)."

21. Of these one-hundred largest US churches, only one is officially part of a Wesleyan

preaching that refuses to acknowledge or embrace the holiness of queer love is, as Wesley says, quoting the Scripture "no better in the judgment of God 'than sounding brass, or a rumbling cymbal.'"[22] Eloquent speech about the Christian faith is meaningless if it has not behind it the love of God that is itself queer and that celebrates love in all its forms.

The gifts of prophecy and knowledge likewise are meaningless if not accompanied by the love of queer folks and queer folks' love. How indeed could one portend to be able to "understand all the mysteries of nature, of providence, and of the Word of God" and yet claim that such mysteries had no relevance to or inclusion of queer life and love?[23] Further, as Wesley says, "though I could explain the most mysterious passages of Daniel, of Ezekiel, and the Revelation; yet if I have not humility, gentleness, and resignation, I am nothing in the sight of God."[24] The supposed knowledge of the Bible, especially, is used against LGBTQ+ Christians in such a way that strips Scripture of its true purpose, which Wesley says elsewhere is always only to point to the loving nature and action of God. When straight, cisgender Christians use the Bible to "clobber" queer folks into agreement or submission, or as some kind of divine "gotcha" to shame LGBTQ+ people into harmful repression, the argument that they are doing so "out of love" holds no water. Even if the most uncharitable reads of the Bible's few mentions of "homosexuality" were somehow "correct" in their condemnations, that is, even if it were the case that we "should" put to death any man who "lies with a man as if with a woman" as it says in Leviticus 20:13, surely we can agree that this would not be loving behavior, and therefore the more loving action (i.e., not killing gay men) should win out. Linn Tonstad considers this point when she discusses enslavement of people in the Bible: "Generally," she says, "people don't need to give all kinds of reasons why slavery is wrong, nor do they spend any time wrestling with the biblical passages that endorse slavery."[25] We know plainly that buying, selling, and owning human beings is not and cannot be done in love—it does not matter that it is presented positively in the Bible or that it was an assumed good. Likewise, the assumed course of action for dealing with what today's readers of the

---

denomination: the United Methodist Church of the Resurrection in Leawood, Kansas, which in 2020 is ranked 27 with an attendance of 9,630.

22. Wesley, *Works* 3:301.

23. Wesley, *Works* 3:301.

24. Wesley, *Works* 3:301.

25. Tonstad, *Queer Theology*, 23.

text might call gay men is plainly not loving. So to have knowledge of such a proposed "fact" of Scripture, and to believe it proper is to be without love, and therefore to be nothing in the sight of God. To be right is worthless when opposed to being loving.

Next, faith. Wesley says that if "faith does not work by love," that is, "if it does not produce universal holiness," then it is useless.[26] This section is perhaps Wesley's most emphatic. "All faith that is, that ever was, or ever can be," Wesley says, "separate from tender benevolence to every child of man, friend or foe, Christian, Jew, heretic, or pagan . . . will stand us in no stead before the face of God."[27] Any faith one has, any belief one holds, will do nothing to help one approach the heart of God unless it is joined by love and care for others, which, of course, is the heart of God itself. What good, then, is a "Bible-believing faith," a "belief in the gospel," or a "faith in Jesus Christ," if it does harm to the LGBTQ+ people it encounters? Wesley is convinced that faith "will never save us from hell unless it now save us from all unholy tempers," which he lists as pride, passion, impatience, arrogance, haughtiness, overbearing, wrath, anger, bitterness, discontent, murmuring, fretfulness, and peevishness.[28] Any queer person who has been involved in a LGBTQ+-rejecting church can tell stories upon stories of such unholy tempers that have been revealed in the course of a conversation about non-normative sexuality. Too many queer young people have seen these unholy tempers emerge from their churchgoing parents once they have come out. In these cases, faith is not producing the love that is holiness, so we must ask: Of what use is this faith?

The Epistle of James says that faith without works is dead. Likewise, Wesley says, are works without love. Wesley criticizes those who do good but for their own egos' sakes, to be praised at their deaths in gaudy, "costly and pompous" funerals.[29] They do not give out of love—how could they when they do not even know the people whom they are benefiting? Love involves real relationship, not the grand, impersonal overtures of "charity work." There are churches that, despite their good intentions of welcoming their LGBTQ+ neighbors, do not truly engage in loving relationship but something more like patronizing pandering. In the same way, aging churches might be greedy to gather young people into their congregations,

26. Wesley, *Works* 3:303.
27. Wesley, *Works* 3:304.
28. Wesley, *Works* 3:304.
29. Wesley, *Works* 3:304.

churches who wish to be seen as progressive might boast rainbow flags or yard signs without doing any of the meaningful, loving work to dismantle systems of cis-heteropatriarchy at play in their institutions. They may welcome LGBTQ+ members without creating truly loving and affirming spaces. They may expect a certain cis-hetero aping or respectability posturing from their queer members, sending the message that it's fine if they're gay, just not *too* gay. Good works are good and look good, but love is real and hard work that often goes unnoticed and unpraised. Forced or expected assimilation to heteronormative society, with its emphasis on monogamous couples, nuclear families, and vanilla sex, is not the ground for loving queer people and our liberation. Doing "good works" for queer folks removed from actual relationship *with* queer folks is not love but only self-service.

Finally, in his most extreme example, Wesley asserts that for a person to suffer persecution and martyrdom, but have not love, is also meaningless. He says that even if a person is killed for their exemplary faith, if they die with resentment or hatred in their heart, they are truly no better than anyone else. The supposed honor of martyrdom is nothing without genuine love of God and neighbor. The perhaps hyperbolic nature of this example serves to emphasize the seriousness of Wesley's position and his read of this text: without real love, even a supposedly noble death is not worth it.

Wesley concludes his sermon with another appeal to the holy tempers sustained by love, saying that the sum is this:

> Whatever I speak, whatever I know, whatever I believe, whatever I do, whatever I suffer; if I have not the faith that worketh by love, that produces love to God and all mankind, I am not in the narrow way which leadeth to life, but in the broad road that leadeth to destruction.[30]

At the end of the day, the only thing that makes the Wesleyan tradition of faith, or any faith at all, worth its salt is love. The core of Wesleyan theology is love. Everything about Wesley's beliefs and teachings on holiness, discipline, Scripture, and God points back to the centrality of love to the Christian life. In this sermon, we see what Wesley has in mind when he reads Paul on love, and how Wesley envisions this love being embodied in Christian community. And the love Wesley expects Christians to embody is definable and demonstrable. It looks like community care and justice and

---

30. Wesley, *Works* 3:306.

honesty and trust and freedom from the consuming toxicity of hatred. It looks like queer love.

LGBTQ+ Christians have so much to teach the church about the creative, wild, prodigal love of God that we can embrace and express as the church here and now. Rather than condemning and castigating queer modes of relationship, the church would do well to listen to queer Christians about the ways they love—each other, themselves, and God—and learn from their experiences.

OF THE CHURCH

Despite his strict discipline and strong opinions, Wesley was, perhaps surprisingly, exceedingly tolerant when it came to issues of doctrine and the unity of the church. His vision holds space for all kinds of beliefs that vary widely and differ with his own. In the midst of his explication of the *one* body, Spirit, hope, Lord, faith, baptism, God and Father of all, it becomes clear that there is indeed not such a one after all. Within this "one" church is a stunning variety of bodies, spirits, faiths that nonetheless coalesce into what we, with Wesley, call a church.

In this chapter, we will explore what church unity might mean when considered through a queer lens, ultimately questioning the tension of unity and diversity, of "one" and "many."

At the end of the first part of this sermon, Wesley uses the text from Ephesians to summarize his answer to the question: What is the church? He says, "The catholic or universal church is all the persons in the universe whom God hath so called out of the world . . . to be 'one body', united by 'one spirit'; having 'one faith, one hope, one baptism, one God and Father of all, who is above all, and through all, and in them all.'"[1] The focus and insistence on oneness is what queerness will question and poke at here, for the queer experience makes us suspicious of such simplicity, such essentialism, such closed finality. Queerness knows, in desire, in love, in expression of the vibrancy of life, there is no reduction to one without the violence of erasure.

In Laurel Schneider's *Beyond Monotheism*, she outlines the enduring Western philosophical myth that she calls "the logic of the One." The logic of the One manifests as obsession with absolutes, with wholeness, with closed and complete systems, with totality and totalitarianism, with

---

1. Wesley, *Works* 3:50.

119

simplicity and consistency and sameness. The logic of the One, or any claim to a single story, is itself a myth—a story that we repeat into a fixed ideology. The story of one, unified, unchanging, and impassible God lends itself to a story of one single and unchangeably correct way of being Christian, of being human. But the reality that shows itself again and again, in the actuality of our lives and experiences, is that such is not the case. As Schneider says, "The logic of the One (and the concept of God that falls within it) is simply *not* One."[2]

Christianity is and always has been syncretistic. From its very Jewish beginnings, and consequent centuries of battles over what might be considered "orthodoxy," to the Reformation, Counter-Reformation, and scores of splits and squabbles since then, it's foolish to think that Christianity has ever been only one thing. There have always been multiple beliefs, practices, interpretations, and rituals, culled from multiple cultures, texts, customs, and traditions. Councils and creeds have done little to quash their abundant and fruitful proliferation. Between the many kinds of Christianities and the many kinds of people who have practiced them and the many kinds of places they have been practiced over the many, many years, the fact of the church's multiplicity is plain.

A queer reading of Wesley's church will look like Schneider's goal of a theology of multiplicity: "a logic, or posture, that resists reduction to the One *and* resists reduction to the Many while affirming a more supple and effective (rather than absolute) unity."[3] It will similarly require the "deconstruction of the logic of the One in pursuit of a postcolonial constructive theology of multiplicity."[4]

Wesley reads the passage in Ephesians about the oneness of the church, and yet even still goes on to acknowledge the diversity within this supposed unity. "I dare not exclude from the church catholic," he declares, "all those congregations in which any unscriptural doctrines . . . are sometimes, yea, frequently preached."[5] This is not even simple diversity, but in fact opposition. Wesley blatantly judges these other congregations as *wrong*, and yet *still* will not exclude them from the "unity" of the church catholic. Such difference is perhaps not what we expect when we think of the conciliatory harmony of unity. This gives an excellent inroad to consider the

2. Schneider, *Beyond Monotheism*, 1

3. Schneider, *Beyond Monotheism*, 5.

4. Schneider, *Beyond Monotheism*, 75.

5. Wesley, *Works* 3:52.

auto-deconstructing properties of unity, in which queerness may function similarly. The queer shows that the straight is never truly straight, just as the One is never just one.

The universal is a clever trick of smoke and mirrors, and even the singular particulars it tries to cover over are never stable. The reality of time and matter means even these queer singularities are shifting from moment to moment. Nothing stands still. To allege a consistent One of any kind is a trap. The center cannot hold.

For each of the particulars Wesley considers from Ephesians—Spirit, hope, Lord, faith, baptism, God, and Father—we can use our tools of queer reading to suss out the multiplicity that actually resides within these supposed "ones."

First, in considering the Spirit, Wesley immediately admits that there are multiple understandings of what this "one" Spirit might be. Some may think it is "the Holy Spirit himself, the fountain of all spiritual life."[6] Even in this first option, the fact that it may be the Holy Spirit, from which is birthed *all* of life, in all of its diverse splendor, hints that this one Spirit is not simply one. Another possibility, Wesley points out, is that it is the Spirit of "spiritual gifts and holy dispositions."[7] Again, how many are such spiritual gifts and dispositions? We must then square "oneness" together with the great variety of gifts and abilities given to the faithful, or of the array of loving dispositions given to the holy.

Next, Wesley asserts one hope—"a hope full of immortality."[8] But is immortality, or that "their prospect extends beyond the grave," really the one, the only hope of the members of the church? Surely the experience of Christ in the hearts and lives of Christians results in multiple types and flavors of hope. We hope for more than an afterlife. We hope for justice, we hope for joy, we hope for peace. We hope for things that can and should come to fruition in this life. We hope for a better life in this world for ourselves, our neighbors, our children. The hope of the Christian life takes many forms, all infused with the love and holiness of God and God's many people. This "one" hope is in no way just one.

There is one Lord, assert Wesley and Ephesians. Yet even as we confess this one Lord as Jesus Christ, the Son of God, is this indeed *one* Lord? Is the Lord we proclaim the self-same Lord proclaimed by Christians in the first,

6. Wesley, *Works* 3:49.

7. Wesley, *Works* 3:49.

8. Wesley, *Works* 3:49.

second, thirteenth centuries? Is it the same Lord proclaimed by the person next to us in the pew? Womanist theologian Jacquelyn Grant's classic text, *White Women's Christ, Black Women's Jesus*, presents the variety of christologies among white feminists ("biblical," "liberationist," and "rejectionist"), and then offers her own womanist critique. Core to this critique is the fact that the experience of white women, whose voices had dominated feminist theology, is different from the experience of Black women and other women of color, and therefore paints a different picture of Christ and the important theologies about him. The insistence on a single hegemonic story about a single white-washed version of Jesus has meant violence upon violence for so much of the world, in both body and spirit. But as we open up to multiple stories and multiple "Jesuses" who bring the gospel of love and justice, we see that the colonial imperative of the One can be dismantled.

There is one faith, but again Wesley distinguishes between different faiths to be clear about which kind he means. The faith he means, and which he reads in Ephesians, is "not barely the faith of a heathen," nor is it "barely the faith of a devil."[9] The heathens and devils, then, do have faith, though a different faith than the Christian faith Wesley is promoting. So we might wonder, if there are multiple kinds of "wrong" faiths—those of heathens as well as those of devils, at least—then why might there not be multiple kinds of right faiths? Is it the case that only one faith will teach us "to say with holy boldness, 'My Lord and my God'"?[10] Even those faiths of the heathen and the devil are not terribly *unlike* the faith of the Christian. According to Wesley, the faith of the Christian just goes further. Wesley says the heathen believes there is a God "and that he is gracious and just, and consequently 'a rewarder of them that diligently seek him.'"[11] The devil believes "all that is written both in the Old and New Testament to be true."[12] In this case, are these faiths then part of the "one" faith that is inclusive of the "right" Christian faith that Wesley affirms? When we look closely, and start asking queer questions and fiddling with words and following threads, we see the logic of the One crumbling before us yet again.

Wesley says there is one baptism, "which is the outward sign our one Lord has been pleased to appoint of all that inward and spiritual grace

---

9. Wesley, *Works* 3:49.

10. Wesley, *Works* 3:49.

11. Wesley, *Works* 3:49. Here Wesley is citing Heb 11:6.

12. Wesley, *Works* 3:49.

which he is continually bestowing upon his church."[13] He gives precious little detail here about what that one baptism is or looks like, though he does have a more expansive "Treatise on Baptism" from 1756. In this essay, Wesley provides an argument for baptism by water in the way of "washing, dipping, or sprinkling; because it is not determined in Scripture in which of these ways it shall be done."[14] He also makes the case for both infant and believer's baptism, saying that both children and adults may be "proper subjects" of baptism. In addition to the multiple methods and subjects of baptism, multiple things occur in baptism. According to Wesley, in baptism the person is cleansed from original sin; enters into covenant with God; enters the church and is made a member of Christ's body; is transformed into a child of God from a child of wrath; and becomes an heir to the kingdom of heaven. Indeed, in his entire treatise, Wesley makes no mention of the "oneness" of baptism or the text from Ephesians 4. With so many ways of baptism, so many people being baptized, and so many effects and actions taking place in baptism, perhaps it is no wonder. What does it mean, then, for there to be one baptism? The variety and multiplicity of the sacrament as it is actually practiced in the world is lost. As Schneider says, "For all of reality [or in this case, baptism] to be 'One,' or subsumed in a One, however, means that all discontinuities, aberrations, and complexity must at some point disappear."[15] If we assert that all of these differences ultimately culminate into the same thing, the same one baptism, then we collapse all of the particularities of difference that are so important to people that they create such fiery conflict.

Finally, Wesley and Ephesians claim that there is one God and Father of all. The One who is God and yet is *also* Father immediately raises the question of "one." To be sure, the trinitarian paradox of God in three Persons actually provides an excellent insight to the need for a more nuanced way of thinking about the universe beyond simple oneness, for indeed in the classical doctrine, God is One, yes, but God is *also* three. To quote Schneider yet again, "the One—whether system, thing, tradition, or God—always fails to be one."[16] The simplicity and finality and limitation of oneness is not enough to hold all of divinity, or all of the church. Marcella Althaus-Reid discusses the queerness of the Trinity in its asymmetry, its

---

13. Wesley, *Works* 3:49.

14. Wesley, *Works of the Rev. John Wesley*, 155.

15. Schneider, *Beyond Monotheism*, 80.

16. Schneider, *Beyond Monotheism*, 138.

refusal to be a one-to-one, monogamous (e.g., God-to-human) relationship. In the introduction of a third, Althaus-Reid says, God "confesses God's primordial non-alignment with Godself."[17] Further, the queer thinking of the Trinity "has proved that God has a back," and "God's back is made of difference."[18] Queer theology is keen to examine God's backside. We wish to see God's back as Moses did, leaving Sinai with his face aglow. God's back, God's shadow-side, God's difference radiates God's glory. In her essay on Althaus-Reid's work, Susannah Cornwall says that "in queering God we must acknowledge God's multiplicity, which flows back into our own."[19] Queer theology refuses to suppress this multiplicity, but instead emphasizes, fosters, and celebrates it. We see the multiplicity in God as we acknowledge it in humanity. *Other*ness is inherent in humanity, in our own selves, in the world, and *yes*, in God. In queer reading, queer theology, and queer life, we set ourselves free to explore and engage this otherness. The queer God can never be simply one.

All of these "onenesses" of the church (so many onenesses!) supposedly point to a unity, a homogenous singularity that is the people of God, the body of Christ. But it's clear that such a body can never be one thing, just as our own individual bodies are made up of trillions of cells, including entire microbiomes of microbes and bacteria. That is, we are at least as microbial as we are human.[20] What makes up *us* is so much not-us. Our bodies themselves are multiple, permeable, and always changing. How much more so the body of Christ, which is made up of so many bodies. Cornwall quotes Grace Jantzen, who points out the importance of Jesus' particularity, saying that "Since Jesus was one man, not all humanity, his incarnation—his being an embodiment of the divine—leaves room for other incarnations, other sexualities, other embodiments."[21] Jesus the man was one body; Jesus the Christ is made up of many. To simplify this queer multiplicity into the singularity of oneness can't help but do violence to the various particularities at stake.

17. Althaus-Reid, *Queer God*, 16.

18. Althaus-Reid, *Queer God*, 16.

19. Cornwall, "Stranger in Our Midst," 102.

20. Abbott, "Scientists Bust Myth That Our Bodies Have More Bacteria than Human Cells." The old, commonly cited figure of bacteria to human cells being 10:1 may be high, but current estimates are still at least 1:1.

21. Cornwall, "Stranger in Our Midst," 107.

When it comes to the church, Wesley's legacy is mixed. We can't forget that, despite his insistence on unity, and his own fierce loyalty to the Church of England, Wesley's work and revivals did ultimately pave the way for the Methodist movement and eventually an entirely new branch of Protestantism. A belief in and commitment to unity does not keep multiplicity from bubbling up and, like yeasty dough, overflowing a too-small bowl.

Some ministers and Christian thinkers talk about the crucial difference between the "bounded set" and the "centered set."[22] In mathematics, a bounded set limits numbers by an upper and a lower boundary that creates a group within the boundary and excludes those numbers outside the boundary. A centered set, on the other hand, has no such boundary but instead is centered on a single point, and numbers are considered in relation to that point. A common understanding of "church unity" often looks like a bounded set: all members hemmed in by the impermeable orthodoxy of correct belief on every side, identifying those within as together against those without. But perhaps a first step toward rethinking church unity against the logic of the One is thinking in terms of the centered set: a diversity of people, with a diversity of beliefs, drawn toward the multiplicitous love of the multiplicitous Christ who is God incarnate. Identifying this "one" center itself as diverse helps us think of unity as a site of diversity. Ultimately, such a model also leads us toward each other—human beings in all our glorious difference.

Unity in the church today must square with and indeed embrace the holy diversity of humanity that reflects the holy diversity of God. And this embrace cannot smother. It must be an embrace toward liberation. An embrace that does not create a boundary. A genial slap on the back for co-travelers on this way that expands out before us toward we-know-not-where.

The second and third parts of the sermon are much shorter.

Part two poses the question: "What is it to 'walk worth of the vocation wherewith we are called'?"[23] How is this "one" unified church to walk, to present itself in the world? The first demand of proper walking, which Wesley says, "includes all our inward and outward motions, all our thoughts, and words, and actions," is "lowliness," or humility.[24] I have discussed in other chapters what a queer reading of humility might mean—that it is not so much thinking of ourselves poorly as much as it is thinking of ourselves

---

22. See, for example, evangelical authors Frost and Hirsch, *Shaping of Things to Come*.

23. Wesley, *Works* 3:53.

24. Wesley, *Works* 3:53.

rightly, that indeed right thinking of ourselves might look more like pride in who we are than like self-denigration. And indeed Wesley says as much here too: to walk "with all lowliness," he says, is "to know ourselves as also we are known by him to whom all hearts are open."[25] True, critical self-awareness is what Wesley determines is required, not naïve or oblivious surrender to a homogenous blob. When we walk as the church, we are to do so with a clear vision of who we are as individuals, in all our queernesses and all our becomings, and we join with others whose desire is likewise to grow into the graces and love of God. This self-awareness, on our own as well as in community, is what continues to guide us in holiness, for, as Wesley says, "How prone is our heart still to depart from the living God! What a tendency to sin remains in our heart, although we know our past sins are forgiven!"[26] The ongoing work of being honestly and openly *ourselves* as we walk together as the church means that a unity of oneness is patently impossible. It means that joining together as the church requires awareness, space, and love for diversity of all kinds.

Next Wesley says walking as the church means to "walk with all meekness," which means having "not only a power over anger, but over all violent and turbulent passions."[27] We'd do well to note that meekness does not necessarily entail an *elimination* of anger or passions, but *power over* them, that is, self-control. Wesley continues, "it implies having all our passions in due proportion; none of them either too strong or too weak, but all duly balanced with each other, all subordinate to reason; and reason directed by the Spirit of God."[28] This need for balance tells us that we have multiple passions at play within us, and that health requires control—not in the sense of suppression but in the sense of ease. For our passions to be too weak is just as much of a problem as for them to be too strong. What's more, this balance falls under the purview of reason, again in the prototypical modernist formulation of reason over emotion. However, the fact that he then in turn subordinates reason to the Spirit allows for an interesting twist. Seeing as the Holy Spirit is perhaps the most tricky, most wily, and most fluid of the three trinitarian Persons, putting one's passions under her guidance may well lead to some surprises. Thinking this way, meekness

25. Wesley, *Works* 3:53. Here Wesley is quoting the Book of Common Prayer's Communion Collect for Purity.

26. Wesley, *Works* 3:53.

27. Wesley, *Works* 3:54.

28. Wesley, *Works* 3:54.

then is not a generalized demure submissiveness, but rather submission to the wild whims of a fiercely loving God of justice, who may call on our various passions in various degrees and various ways. Moreover, we must again acknowledge the particularity of the individuals who make up this church, and their unique makeups and balances of passions and abilities. There is so much constant movement and flux of attitude and affect and emotion swirling in and between these innumerable bodies and directed by the Spirit, to attempt to contain them into a unity of "meekness" would be foolhardy indeed.

The last two marks Wesley identifies as part of the church's walking together are long-suffering and forbearance.[29] The patience and tolerance required in these characteristics make all too clear the differences, disagreements, and conflicts at play, both between members of the church and when in relationship with others outside of it. The long-suffering of the church and those who make up the church, Wesley says, "though provoked ever so often, it is still the same, quiet and unshaken."[30] This peace and patience is not a result of coming to agreement or having differences stamped out or conquered. It is a welcoming of discomfort, of questions, of inconsistencies, because in those conflicts is where we find our most truthful reality. The "forbearing one another in love" that Wesley talks about is, he says, "not only the not resenting anything, and the not avenging yourselves; not only the not injuring, hurting, or grieving each other, either by word or deed; but also the bearing one another's burdens."[31] How hard it seems for us to do the former, not to mention the latter. How much the church has injured, hurt, and grieved its queer members! So many of the burdens LGBTQ+ Christians must bear are inflicted by other Christians, in the name of the very community that should be easing their pain in an antagonistic world. Surely the patience and tolerance toward one another that Wesley here prescribes should be extended to all of our siblings in Christ, to all of God's vibrant and diverse children, and most especially to those most often harmed and marginalized among us.

The third and final part of the sermon is a short conclusion, summarizing what it means for the members of the church—and who exactly such people are—to "keep the unity of the Spirit in the bond of peace."[32] Wesley

---

29. Wesley, *Works* 3:54–55.

30. Wesley, *Works* 3:54.

31. Wesley, *Works* 3:55.

32. Wesley, *Works* 3:55.

asserts that the unity of the church comes essentially from its holiness—that it, like the God who calls its members and like the members themselves, is holy, and therefore in a unity of peace. Given what we have already discussed above about the logic of the One at play in common understandings of unity, how can we think a multiplicitous unity in relation to holiness? Wesley himself actually hints at the diversity of holiness in the church, saying, "[E]very member [of the church] is holy, though in different degrees."[33] The journey of holiness in the life of each individual, that is, how they specifically grow and become more perfect in their love of God and neighbor, is as unique as that individual. Holiness itself cannot be one thing, given that it is based on love, which is always inherently contextual and particular. So while certainly those who are not attuned to and striving for holy love inwardly and outwardly in their lives (Wesley lists some who he considers examples of such resistance) may not be considered members of the church, there are so many kinds of people and ways of being that yet should be.

Ultimately, to queer Wesley, and to queer the church, is to open ourselves to the reality of multiplicity in ourselves and our communities. The "unity" that we project on faith, the church, God, and even our own bodies is at its core a myth—a story that perpetuates the "logic of the One" that in turn upholds the systems of oppression, repression, and violence that actually push us further from holiness. What if we were to release this stranglehold we often call "church unity" so that we could consider the church as a more capacious, breathable space? What if we thought of the church less like a bounded set and more like a centered set, drawing all kinds of people together in love toward God who is Godself multiple in oneness? What if our humility and meekness and patience, which mark us outwardly as members of the church, were not about shaving ourselves down to fit into some prescribed box called "unity," but rather were about exploding out into loving relationship upon loving relationship, with ourselves, with others, and with God? What if right thinking of ourselves, submission to the Holy Spirit, and tolerance of others and their journeys were what marked us as members of the church? A Wesleyan theology of multiplicity can be a promising way forward toward a queer, liberating holiness that is our inheritance.

---

33. Wesley, *Works* 3:55–56.

CONCLUSIONS

John Wesley was not a systematician, and neither am I. Theology and spirituality and the material stuff of life itself are far too messy and sticky and downright weird for any of it to be domesticated into a forthright, airtight structure. Our manuals and books of discipline and *Robert's Rules of Order* are nice, and can help us feel a sense of control and orthodoxy in our churches and our lives, but at the end of the day the realities of complex people and emotions and bodies and the surprising and unpredictable ways of a wily Spirit and prodigal God will never be settled and systematized.

Ultimately, to read Wesley queerly is to read *with* Wesley *against* Wesley. As Methodist liberation theologian José Míguez Bonino says, Latin American liberation theologians "are increasingly claiming their right to 'mis-read' their teachers, to find their own insertion in the theological tradition, to offer their own interpretation of the theological task."[1] The act of deliberately "mis-reading" your teachers in order to birth your own method and mode of thought is a standard and necessary part of the process of scholarship, including theology. True critical scholarship with an eye toward progress will split the difference between unquestioning hero worship and wholesale rejection. We take what we can, what is useful and fruitful for pioneering into the future, and we rethink and rework the rest as needed. A Wesleyan posture of grace and love and holiness allows us to deconstruct Wesley himself—to find his inconsistencies, to question his assumptions, to hold his words up to the sunlight of the present, through hundreds of years of struggle and knowledge and change. We read Wesley as Wesleyans who value current science, who work in solidarity with the poor, who see love as the utmost calling of holiness. Reading Wesley as Wesleyans means we read dynamically, seeing his words not as an unmovable foundation but

---

1. Bonino, *Doing Theology in a Revolutionary Situation*, 62.

as a springy jumping-off point that allows us to integrate more fully the faith of our tradition and the lives we live today. Wesley himself, despite his tendency toward order and rigidity, was always open to learning, growing, and changing. He pushed himself in the progress toward perfection. By reading these sermons from a queer, twenty-first-century perspective, we are able to see them in a way that can have real, concrete impact for people in our churches and the way they are welcomed. We are able to see them in a way that is faithful to our Wesleyan heritage and also takes seriously the struggles and injustices faced by LGBTQ+ people. And we are able to see that Wesleyan faith and queer life do not have to be in conflict.

In fact, queer life has so much to offer the world and the church if we would consider it seriously, curiously, and humbly rather than reject outright anyone whose gender expression, sexuality, or relational configuration diverged a modicum from the compulsory norms. There is much to learn from the challenges of queer folks, particularly queer Christians, in their journeys to confront, question, and explore their desires and identities despite an entire society pressuring them to fall in line with the rules of cis-heteropatriarchal supremacy. The repressive, oppressive expectations and assumptions, which the church has chosen to uphold rather than abolish, serve only to privilege a few with power while the rest must unjustly struggle for lives of joy and dignity. However, we know that God is always on the side of the marginalized and always on the side of love. And we know that love is the center of holiness—both God's holiness and the holiness of Christian perfection. So we must consider the real, significant contributions that a liberatory queer theology can offer the Wesleyan tradition and the church at large. What's more, such a theology does not have to be a complete divergence from the roots of our beliefs and practices, but instead can be entirely consistent with the *ethos* of Wesley's work and legacy.

Wesleyan theology and Wesleyan community are ripe for proper engagement with queer theory and LGBTQ+ Christians. The fear that has until now dominated the discussions and work of queer people in the church, silencing their voices and dampening their spirits, is not of God. As Wesleyans in pursuit of Christian perfection, of perfect love of God and neighbor, we must remember that such perfect love casts out fear, and we have nothing to fear from our queer friends and siblings. The diverse love of queer folks gives us so much rich material to work with as we consider ways of loving our neighbors and resisting against oppressive and sinful structures in our world. Queer experience can open our minds, hearts, and lives to possibilities of thought, emotion, and care that go beyond the staid, claustrophobia-inducing prescriptions of cis-heteronormativity. Surely, the Wesleyan emphasis on love in our theology and ecclesial life should be excited by and encouraging of the expansive explosion of love and potentiality that queer thinking and living offers us. Surely, the Wesleyan care for the marginalized and value of broad inclusion should mean there is space for LGBTQ+ people in our churches and our theology. Surely, it's time for serious queer work in our Wesleyan churches.

At the end of the day, the foundation that John Wesley left us through his journals, notes, essays, and especially sermons is meant to be built upon. Much building has been done already to engage in constructive Wesleyan thought about women, race, class, economics, and other important contextual theologies. However, critical work using Wesleyan theology to consider gender and sexuality seems still not to have begun.

My hope is that this project can serve as a springboard for conversations toward a robust queer Wesleyan theology that is both unapologetically queer and faithfully Wesleyan. A queer reading of Wesley's sermons reveals those places of compatibility between the two, as well as those places of conflict we must confront as we continue on in the twenty-first century. It will not serve the church, as individuals or as a corporate body, to pretend that we can live within the mindset of hundreds of years ago, much less thousands. If we desire to maintain a connection to our tradition, this tradition must be one that also embraces the changes of the future. It must be able to adapt and flow as a continuous stream, not dammed up by bigotry and fear. It must welcome the varieties of embodiment and love fought for and experienced by the people who claim it and live within it.

Like any theology undertaken for the good of the church, a queer Wesleyan theology will be a labor of community, a promiscuous effort of trial and error, of fooling around and fumbling in the dark together. We are at the beginning of this relationship, and I am excited—truly giddy with anticipation. My stomach flutters to think about the possibilities for queer Wesleyans and the Wesleyan churches as they begin to collaborate in the holy love we are called to in Jesus Christ. The creative and life-giving work is ahead of us, and I can only imagine what a lovely and just and beautiful world we can shape once we begin queering Wesley and queering the church.

BIBLIOGRAPHY

Abbott, Alison. "Scientists Bust Myth That Our Bodies Have More Bacteria than Human Cells." *Nature News*, January 8, 2016. https://doi.org/10.1038/nature.2016.19136.

Albrecht-Samarasinha, Leah Lilith. "On Being a Bisexual Femme." In *Femme: Feminists, Lesbians and Bad Girls*, edited by Laura Harris and Elizabeth Crocker, 136–44. New York: Routledge, 1997.

Althaus-Reid, Marcella. *Indecent Theology: Theological Perversions in Sex, Gender and Politics*. London: Routledge, 2001.

———. *The Queer God*. New York: Routledge, 2003.

Barad, Karen. *Meeting the Universe Halfway: Quantum Physics and the Entanglement of Matter and Meaning*. Durham: Duke University Press, 2007.

———. "Nature's Queer Performativity." *Qui Parle* 19.2 (2011) 121–58.

Bataille, Georges. *Erotism: Death and Sensuality*. Translated by Mary Dalwood. Reprint, San Francisco: City Lights, 1986.

Bersani, Leo. "Is the Rectum a Grave?" *October* 43 (1987) 197–222. https://doi.org/10.2307/3397574.

Betcher, Sharon V. *Spirit and the Obligation of Social Flesh: A Secular Theology for the Global City*. New York: Fordham University Press, 2014.

Blackwood, Evelyn. "From Butch-Femme to Female Masculinities: Elizabeth Kennedy and LGBT Anthropology." *Feminist Formations* 24.3 (2012) 92–100.

Bonino, José Míguez. *Doing Theology in a Revolutionary Situation*. Philadelphia: Fortress, 1975.

The Book of Discipline of the United Methodist Church. Nashville: United Methodist, 2016.

Boyarin, Daniel. *A Radical Jew: Paul and the Politics of Identity*. Berkeley: University of California Press, 1994.

Brown, Lea D. "Dancing in the Eros of Domination and Submission." In *Dancing Theology in Fetish Boots: Essays in Honour of Marcella Althaus-Reid*, edited by Lisa Isherwood and Mark D. Jordan, 141–52. London: SCM, 2010.

Butler, Judith. "Performative Acts and Gender Constitution: An Essay in Phenomenology and Feminist Theory." *Theatre Journal* 40.4 (1988) 519–31. https://doi.org/10.2307/3207893.

Chauncey, George. *Gay New York: Gender, Urban Culture, and the Making of the Gay Male World, 1890–1940*. New York: Basic Books, 2008.

Cheng, Patrick S. *From Sin to Amazing Grace*. New York: Seabury, 2012.

———. *Radical Love: An Introduction to Queer Theology*. New York: Seabury, 2011.

Cornwall, Susannah. "Stranger in Our Midst: The Becoming of the Queer God in the Theology of Marcella Althaus-Reid." In *Dancing Theology in Fetish Boots: Essays in Honour of Marcella Althaus-Reid*, edited by Lisa Isherwood and Mark D. Jordan, 95–112. London: SCM, 2010.

Crosby, Frances. "Blessed Assurance." In *The United Methodist Hymnal*, no. 369. Nashville: United Methodist, 1989.

Douglas, Kelly B. *Sexuality and the Black Church: A Womanist Perspective*. Maryknoll: Orbis, 1999.

Edman, Elizabeth M. *Queer Virtue: What LGBTQ People Know about Life and Love and How It Can Revitalize Christianity*. Boston: Beacon, 2016.

Farley, Wendy. *Gathering Those Driven Away: A Theology of Incarnation*. Louisville: Westminster John Knox, 2011.

Fausto-Sterling, Anne. *Sex/Gender: Biology in a Social World*. New York: Routledge, 2012.

Fergusson, David M., et al. "Is Sexual Orientation Related to Mental Health Problems and Suicidality in Young People?" *Archives of General Psychiatry* 56.10 (October 1, 1999) 876–80. https://doi.org/10.1001/archpsyc.56.10.876.

Forsaith, Peter S. "'. . . too indelicate to mention . . .': Transgressive Male Sexualities in Early Methodism." *Methodist Review* 12 (February 10, 2020) 61–84.

Foucault, Michel. *The History of Sexuality*. Vol. 1, *An Introduction*. Translated by Robert Hurley. New York: Vintage, 1990.

Frost, Michael, and Alan Hirsch. *The Shaping of Things to Come: Innovation and Mission for the 21 Century Church*. Peabody: Hendrickson, 2003.

Goldstein, Valerie Saiving. "The Human Situation: A Feminine View." *The Journal of Religion* 40.2 (1960) 100–12.

Grant, Jacquelyn. *White Women's Christ and Black Women's Jesus: Feminist Christology and Womanist Response*. American Academy of Religion Academy Series 64. Atlanta: Scholars, 1989.

Grider, J. Kenneth. *A Wesleyan-Holiness Theology*. Kansas City: Beacon, 1994.

Gudorf, Christine E. *Body, Sex, and Pleasure: Reconstructing Christian Sexual Ethics*. Cleveland: Pilgrim, 1994.

Hall, Donald. "BI-Ntroduction II." In *RePresenting BiSexualities: Subjects and Cultures of Fluid Desire*, edited by Donald Hall and Maria Pramaggiore, 8–17. New York: New York University Press, 1996.

Hamblin, Rebecca, and Alan M. Gross. "Role of Religious Attendance and Identity Conflict in Psychological Well-Being." *Journal of Religion and Health* 52.3 (September 1, 2013) 817–27. https://doi.org/10.1007/s10943-011-9514-4.

Iovino, Joe. "What Happened and What Didn't at General Conference 2019." *The People of the United Methodist Church*, March 4, 2019. https://www.umc.org/en/content/what-happened-and-what-didnt-at-general-conference-2019.

Isherwood, Lisa. *The Power of Erotic Celibacy: Queering Heteropatriarchy*. London: T&T Clark, 2006.

Isherwood, Lisa, and Dorothea McEwan, eds. *Introducing Feminist Theology*. Sheffield: Academic, 1993.

Johnson, Jay Emerson. *Peculiar Faith: Queer Theology for Christian Witness*. New York: Seabury, 2014.

Jordan, Mark D. *The Ethics of Sex*. Oxford: Wiley-Blackwell, 2002.

———. *The Invention of Sodomy in Christian Theology*. Chicago: University of Chicago Press, 1997.

Kamitsuka, Margaret. "Sexual Pleasure." In *The Oxford Handbook of Theology, Sexuality, and Gender*, edited by Adrian Thatcher, 505–22. Oxford: Oxford University Press, 2015.

Kennedy, Elizabeth Lapovsky, and Madeline D. Davis. *Boots of Leather, Slippers of Gold*. New York: Routledge, 1993.

Kwok, Pui-Lan. *Postcolonial Imagination and Feminist Theology*. Louisville: Westminster John Knox, 2005.

Leclerc, Diane. *Singleness of Heart: Gender, Sin, and Holiness in Historical Perspective*. Lanham: Scarecrow, 2001.

Lightsey, Pamela R. *Our Lives Matter: A Womanist Queer Theology*. Eugene: Pickwick, 2015.

Lorde, Audre. "Uses of the Erotic." In *Sister Outsider*, 53–59. Reprint, Berkeley: Crossing, 2007.

Marquardt, Manfred. *John Wesley's Social Ethics: Praxis and Principles*. Nashville: Abingdon, 1992.

Marshal, Michael P., et al. "Suicidality and Depression Disparities Between Sexual Minority and Heterosexual Youth: A Meta-Analytic Review." *Journal of Adolescent Health* 49.2 (August 1, 2011) 115–23. https://doi.org/10.1016/j.jadohealth.2011.02.005.

Martin, Dale B. "Arsenokoites and Malakos: Meanings and Consequences." In *Biblical Ethics and Homosexuality*, edited by Robert L. Brawley, 117–36. Louisville: Westminster John Knox, 1996.

McEwan, David. "'I Am Yet Persuaded, You Do Greatly Err': Whitefield, Wesley, and Christian Perfection." In *Wesley and Whitefield? Wesley Versus Whitefield?*, edited by Ian Maddock, 87–104. Eugene: Pickwick, 2018.

Moon, Dawne. *God, Sex, and Politics: Homosexuality and Everyday Theologies*. Chicago: University of Chicago Press, 2004.

Norton, Rictor. *Myth of the Modern Homosexual: Queer History and the Search for Cultural Unity*. London: Bloomsbury, 2016.

Oliveto, Karen P. *Our Strangely Warmed Hearts: Coming Out into God's Call*. Nashville: Abingdon, 2018.

———. *Together at the Table*. Louisville: Westminster John Knox, 2018.

Plessis, Michael du. "Blatantly Bisexual; or, Unthinking Queer Theory." In *RePresenting BiSexualities*, edited by Donald Hall and Maria Pramaggiore, 19–54. New York: New York University Press, 1996.

Powell, Samuel M. *Holiness in the 21st Century*. San Diego: Point Loma, 2004.

Ruether, Rosemary Radford. "Talking Dirty, Speaking Truth." In *Dancing Theology in Fetish Boots: Essays in Honour of Marcella Althaus-Reid*, edited by Lisa Isherwood and Mark D. Jordan, 254–67. London: SCM, 2010.

Rodriguez, Eric M., and Suzanne C. Ouellette. "Gay and Lesbian Christians: Homosexual and Religious Identity Integration in the Members and Participants of a Gay-Positive Church." *Journal for the Scientific Study of Religion* 39.3 (2000) 333–47. https://doi.org/10.1111/0021-8294.00028.

Sandoval, Gaby. "Passing Loquería." In *Femme: Feminists, Lesbians and Bad Girls*, edited by Laura Harris and Elizabeth Crocker, 170–74. New York: Routledge, 1997.

Schneider, Laurel. *Beyond Monotheism: A Theology of Multiplicity*. New York: Routledge, 2007.

Schoene, Berthold. "Queer Politics, Queer Theory, and the Future Of 'Identity': Spiralling out of Culture." In *The Cambridge Companion to Feminist Literary Theory*, edited by Ellen Rooney, 283–302. Cambridge Companions to Literature. Cambridge: Cambridge University Press, 2006. doi:10.1017/CCOL0521807069.014.

"Scoring America's 100 Largest Churches for Clarity (2017)." *Church Clarity*, March 25, 2019. https://www.churchclarity.org/resources/scoring-americas-100-largest-churches-for-clarity.

Spade, Dean, and Craig Willse. "Marriage Will Never Set Us Free." *Organizing Upgrade*, 2013. https://archive.organizingupgrade.com/index.php/modules-menu/beyond-capitalism/item/1002-marriage-will-never-set-us-free.

Tonstad, Linn Marie. *Queer Theology: Beyond Apologetics*. Eugene: Cascade, 2018.

Wesley, John. *The Works of John Wesley*. Edited by Albert Outler. 4 vols. Nashville: Abingdon, 1985.

———. *The Works of the Rev. John Wesley: The Doctrine of Original Sin, and Tracts on Various Subjects of Polemical Divinity*. New York: J. & J. Harper, 1827.

Williford, Daniel. "Queer Aesthetics." *Borderlands* 8.2 (October 2009).

Wink, Walter. "Biblical Perspectives on Homosexuality." *The Christian Century* 96.36 (November 7, 1979) 1082–86.

Wolff, Joshua R., et al. "Sexual Minority Students in Non-Affirming Religious Higher Education: Mental Health, Outness, and Identity." *Psychology of Sexual Orientation and Gender Diversity* 3.2 (June 2016) 201–12. http://dx.doi.org.proxy.library.vanderbilt.edu/10.1037/sgd0000162.

Wynkoop, Mildred Bangs. *A Theology of Love: The Dynamic of Wesleyanism*. Kansas City, MO: Beacon Hill, 1972.

CPSIA information can be obtained
at www.ICGtesting.com
Printed in the USA
LVHW111759260721
693719LV00001B/22